We live in a time of alarming ignorance of the bedrock and transformational doctrines of the Christian faith. *Foundations* was crafted in response to the growing need for believers to learn, love, and live the timeless truths of Scripture.

—DR. KENNETH BOA, PRESIDENT, REFLECTIONS MINISTRIES

In an age when Bible doctrine is devalued, Tom Holladay and Kay Warren have coauthored a seminal work that has come to the kingdom for such a time as ours. *Foundations*, a well-devised tool with realistic learning levels in mind, will equip a new generation of informed believers. A biblical theology linked with practical relevance.

—HOWARD G. HENDRICKS, DISTINGUISHED PROFESSOR AND CHAIRMAN, DALLAS THEOLOGICAL SEMINARY

At last! A curriculum that will root hearts and heads in the solid ground of God's Word in a way that makes sense in this complex and challenging world. These studies are targeted to empower teachers and leaders to mentor others toward purpose, potential, and fruitfulness! I am thrilled to recommend it!

—DR. JOSEPH M. STOWELL, PRESIDENT, MOODY BIBLE INSTITUTE

This excellent curriculum shouts its message from the housetops that if the truth is broken down into small pieces so that all may read, mark, and inwardly digest it, it will be sweeter than honey, like fire in the bones of those who commit themselves to learn it. Never has our crazy world so needed such help.

—JILL BRISCOE, AUTHOR

Tom Holladay and Kay Warren have designed a winsome and accessible introduction to the basic beliefs of the Christian faith. It will be a gift both to those who teach and those who learn.

—JOHN ORTBERG, TEACHING PASTOR, MENLO PARK PRESBYTERIAN CHURCH

How refreshing to find a book on doctrine (often a dusty subject) that's down-to-earth, easy to grasp, with great illustrations and humor to boot! This is one book that makes the study of doctrine come alive.

—JUNE HUNT, AUTHOR

I can't affirm the value of this type of resource too strongly. Growth without depth and building without a foundation are two surefire approaches to delusion, disappointment, and eventual defeat, if not destruction. Thank God for the foresight as well as the insight that Tom Holladay and Kay Warren have shown in serving us with *Foundations*.

—JACK HAYFORD, INTERNATIONALLY KNOWN AUTHOR AND SPEAKER

Tom Holladay and Kay Warren have done for us and our churches what we all know we need to do—get people grounded in the core doctrines of the faith. As important as touching people's felt needs are to evangelism, so equally important is the grasping of biblical truth in a refreshing and applicational manner to discipleship. *Foundations* is the systematic, doctrinally sound, and applicationally relevant resource we've all been waiting for. Great work, Tom and Kay! I highly recommend it.

—CHIP INGRAM, PRESIDENT/CEO WALK THRU THE BIBLE

Thank God for Tom Holladay and Kay Warren! Their new curriculum, *Foundations,* is a powerful resource for anyone wanting to strengthen their understanding of basic Christian doctrine and build their lives on the foundation of truth. This twenty-four-session study in systematic theology for lay people has been completed by more than 3,000 members of Saddleback Church, as well as a number of other churches, and it is bound to change people's lives forever!

—JOSH D. MCDOWELL, AUTHOR AND SPEAKER

Tom Holladay and Kay Warren have given us a proven tool for one of the most vital needs in today's world— *Foundations*. This study answers the need of Christians who need a skeleton of biblical truth to support them. God will bless you and your church through this very practical and personal study of God's Word.

—AVERY WILLIS, SENIOR VICE PRESIDENT, OVERSEAS OPERATIONS, INTERNATIONAL MISSION BOARD

At last! This curriculum supplies the missing link in the study of theology by demonstrating on every page that theology is about life. Kay Warren and Tom Holladay have done us all a favor by removing the password protection from theology and making it accessible, inviting, and understandable for every Christian and by showing us how down-to-earth and practical knowing God can be. I highly recommend it!

—CAROLYN CUSTIS JAMES, INTERNATIONAL CONFERENCE SPEAKER AND AUTHOR OF *WHEN LIFE AND BELIEFS COLLIDE*

Tom and Kay are not content in producing converts. They are committed to turning converts into reproducing disciplemakers through time-tested truths presented in an accessible format.

—HANK HANEGRAAFF, HOST OF THE *BIBLE ANSWER MAN*

Foundations provides a thorough study of the core truths of the Christian faith. In a day when there is much confusion over what Christians really believe, this curriculum anchors the believer solidly in truth.

—STEPHEN ARTERBURN, FOUNDER AND CHAIRMAN, NEW LIFE MINISTRIES

Tom Holladay is a teaching pastor at Saddleback Church in Lake Forest, California. With Kay Warren, he developed the *Foundations* curriculum to teach in-depth doctrine to the largely unchurched congregation. In addition to his pastoral leadership and weekend teaching duties at Saddleback, Tom assists Rick Warren in teaching Purpose-Driven® Church conferences to Christian leaders all over the world. He and his wife, Chaundel, have three children.

Kay Warren is a teacher at Purpose-Driven events and other conferences around the world. She and her husband, Rick, began Saddleback Church in their home in 1980 with seven people. The church has since grown to become one of the largest in America and one of the most influential in the world. A mother of three children, Kay is also a Bible teacher and an advocate for women and children affected by HIV/AIDS.

11 CORE TRUTHS TO BUILD YOUR LIFE ON

foundations

A PURPOSE-DRIVEN® DISCIPLESHIP RESOURCE

Participant's Guide

tom HoLLaDay & kay waRReN

ZONDERVAN™
GRAND RAPIDS, MICHIGAN 49530 USA

We want to hear from you. Please send your comments about this book to us in care of zreview@zondervan.com. Thank you.

ZONDERVAN™

Foundations Participant's Guide
Copyright © 2003 by Tom Holladay and Kay Warren

Requests for information should be addressed to:
Zondervan, *Grand Rapids, Michigan 49530*

ISBN: 0-310-24073-5

Interior design by Beth Shagene

Printed in the United States of America

06 07 08 09 /❖ VG/ 10

Contents

Foreword

What *Foundations* Will Do for You

I once built a log cabin in the Sierra mountains of northern California. After ten backbreaking weeks of clearing forest land, all I had to show for my effort was a leveled and squared concrete foundation. I was discouraged, but my father, who built over a hundred church buildings in his lifetime, said, "Cheer up, son! Once you've laid the foundation, the most important work is behind you." I've since learned that this is a principle for all of life: you can never build *anything* larger than the foundation can handle.

The foundation of any building determines both its size and strength, and the same is true of our lives. A life built on a false or faulty foundation will never reach the height that God intends for it to reach. If you skimp on your foundation, you limit your life.

That's why this material is so vitally important. *Foundations* is the biblical basis of the Purpose-Driven Life. You *must* understand these life-changing truths to enjoy God's purposes for you. This curriculum has been taught, tested, and refined over ten years with thousands of people at Saddleback Church. I've often said that Foundations is the most important class in our church.

Why You Need a Biblical Foundation for Life

- *It's the source of personal growth and stability.* So many of the problems in our lives are caused by faulty thinking. That's why Jesus said the truth will set us free and why Colossians 2:7 says, "Plant your roots in Christ and let him be the foundation for your life" (CEV).

- *It's the underpinning of a healthy family.* Proverbs 24:3 says, "Homes are built on the foundation of wisdom and understanding" (TEV). In a world that is constantly changing, strong families are based on God's unchanging truth.

- *It's the starting point of leadership.* You can never lead people farther than you've gone yourself. Proverbs 16:12 says, "Sound leadership has a moral foundation" (MESSAGE).

- *It's the basis for your eternal reward in heaven.* Paul said, "Whatever we build on that foundation will be tested by fire on the day of judgment. . . . We will be rewarded if our building is left standing" (1 Cor. 3:12–14 CEV).

- *God's truth is the only foundation that will last.* The Bible tells us that "the sound, wholesome teachings of the Lord Jesus Christ . . . are the foundation for a godly life" (1 Tim. 6:3 NLT) and that "God's truth stands firm like a foundation stone" (2 Tim. 2:19 NLT).

Jesus concluded his Sermon on the Mount with a story illustrating this important truth. Two houses were built on different foundations. The house built on sand was destroyed when rain, floods, and wind swept it away. But the house built on the foundation of solid rock remained firm. He concluded, "Therefore everyone who hears these words of mine and puts them into practice is like the wise man who built his house on the rock" (Matt. 7:24). The MESSAGE paraphrase of this verse shows how important this is: "These words I speak to you are not incidental additions to your life. . . . They are foundational words, words to build a life on."

I cannot recommend this curriculum more highly to you. It has changed our church, our staff, and thousands of lives. For too long, too many have thought of theology as something that doesn't relate to our everyday lives, but *Foundations* explodes that mold. This study makes it clear that the foundation of what we do and say in each day of our lives is what we believe. I am thrilled that this in-depth, life-changing curriculum is now being made available for everyone to use.

—RICK WARREN, AUTHOR OF *THE PURPOSE-DRIVEN LIFE*

Bring It to Life!

Get ready for a radical statement, a pronouncement sure to make you wonder if we've lost our grip on reality. *There is nothing more exciting than doctrine!*

Track with us for a second on this. Doctrine is the study of what God has to say. What God has to say is always the truth. The truth gives me the right perspective on myself and on the world around me. The right perspective results in decisions of faith and experiences of joy. *That* is exciting!

The objective of *Foundations* is to present the basic truths of the Christian faith in a simple, systematic, and life-changing way. In other words, to teach doctrine. The question is, Why? In a world in which people's lives are filled with crying needs, why teach doctrine? Because biblical doctrine has the answer to many of those crying needs! Please don't see this as a clash between needs-oriented and doctrine-oriented teaching. The truth is we need both. We all need to learn how to deal with worry in our lives. One of the keys to dealing with worry is an understanding of the biblical doctrine of the hope of heaven. Couples need to know what the Bible says about how to have a better marriage. They also need a deeper understanding of the doctrine of the Fatherhood of God, giving the assurance of God's love upon which all healthy relationships are built. Parents need to understand the Bible's practical insights for raising kids. They also need an understanding of the sovereignty of God, a certainty of the fact that God is in control that will carry them through the inevitable ups and downs of being a parent. Doctrinal truth meets our deepest needs.

Welcome to a study that will have a lifelong impact on the way that you look at everything around you and above you and within you. As the writers of this study, our goal is to help you to develop a "Christian worldview." A Christian worldview is the ability to see everything through the filter of God's truth. The time that you dedicate to this study will lay a foundation for new perspectives that will have tremendous benefits for the rest of your life. This study will help you to:

- Lessen the stress in everyday life
- See the real potential for growth that the Lord has given you
- Increase your sense of security in an often troubling world

- Find new tools for helping others (your friends, your family, your children) find the right perspective on life
- Fall more deeply in love with the Lord

Throughout this study you'll see four types of sidebar sections designed to help you connect with the truths that God tells us about himself, ourselves, and this world.

- *A Fresh Word:* One aspect of doctrine that makes people "nervous" is the "big words." Throughout this study we'll take a fresh look at these words, words such as *omnipotent* and *sovereign.*
- *A Closer Look:* We'll take time to expand on a truth or to look at it from a different perspective.
- *Key Personal Perspective:* The truth of doctrine always has a profound impact on our lives. In these sections we'll focus in on that personal impact.
- *Acting on the Truth:* James 1:22 says, "Do what God's teaching says; when you only listen and do nothing, you are fooling yourselves" (NCV).

Memory cards: Your guide also includes a memory card for each of the eleven core truths in this study. Each card states the essence of the doctrine on one side, with a key verse concerning that doctrine on the other side.

Discussion questions. You'll find Discussion Questions at the end of each study.

Get ready for God to do incredible things in your life as you begin the adventure of learning more deeply about the most exciting message in the world: the truth about God!

Introductory Study

Life Change Objectives

- To trust in the power of God's truth to change your life.

- To anticipate in faith the changes that learning doctrine will make in you.

Developing a Christian Worldview

And this is my prayer: that your love may abound more and more in knowledge and depth of insight, so that you may be able to discern what is best.

—Philippians 1:9–10

But you, dear friends, must continue to build your lives on the foundation of your holy faith.

—Jude 1:20(NLT)

A Fresh Word

What Is Christian Doctrine?

- Christian doctrine is an _____
  of what the _____ about the most
  important issues of life.

- A working definition of theology is: _____
  _____.

Why Learn Doctrine?

Because knowing the truth about God helps me

_____

We are cruel to ourselves if we try to live in this world without knowing the God whose world it is and who runs it. The world becomes a strange, mad, painful place . . . for those who do not know about God.[1]

—J. I. Packer

Listen carefully to wisdom; set your mind on understanding. Cry out for wisdom, and beg for understanding. Search for it like silver, and hunt for it like hidden treasure. Then you will understand respect for the LORD, and you will find that you know God.

—Proverbs 2:2–5 (NCV)

Knowing God will make you wise;
Knowing God will open your eyes;
Knowing God will give you hope;
Knowing God will help you cope.

—Kay Warren

Because knowledge is an _____

Therefore leaving the elementary teaching about the Christ, let us press on to maturity, not laying again the foundation of repentance from dead works and of faith toward God, of instructions [doctrine] about washings [baptism], and laying on of hands, and the resurrection of the dead, and eternal judgment.

—Hebrews 6:1–2 (NASB)

Life without a foundation

. . . until we all reach unity in the faith and in the knowledge of the Son of God and become mature, attaining to the whole measure of the fullness of Christ. Then we will no longer be infants, tossed back and forth by the waves, and blown here and there by every wind of teaching and by the cunning and craftiness of men in their deceitful scheming.

—Ephesians 4:13–14

1. "Tossed back and forth by the waves . . ."

   Without truth I am vulnerable to _____.

2. "Blown here and there by every wind of teaching . . ."

   Without truth I am victimized by _____.

Life with a foundation

Therefore everyone who hears these words of mine and puts them into practice is like a wise man who built his house on the rock. The rain came down, the streams rose, and the winds blew and beat against that house; yet it did not fall, because it had its foundation on the rock.

—Matthew 7:24–25

Because doctrine feeds my soul

In pointing out these things to the brethren, you will be a good servant of Christ Jesus, constantly nourished on the words of the faith and of the sound doctrine which you have been following.

—1 Timothy 4:6 (NASB)

For though by this time you ought to be teachers, you have need again for someone to teach you the elementary principles of the oracles of God, and you have come to need milk and not solid food. For everyone who partakes *only* of milk is not accustomed to the word of righteousness, for he is a babe. But solid food is for the mature.

—Hebrews 5:12–14 (NASB)

And now I commend you to God and to the word of His grace, which is able to build you up.

—Acts 20:32 (NASB)

Because knowing the truth enables me to serve others

If you give these instructions to the believers, you will be a good servant of Christ Jesus, as you feed yourself spiritually on the words of faith and of the true teaching which you have followed.

—1 Timothy 4:6 (GNT)

He must hold firmly to the trustworthy message as it has been taught, so that he can encourage others by sound doctrine and refute those who oppose it.

Titus 1:9

Because knowing the truth protects against error

So then, just as you received Christ Jesus as Lord, continue to live in him, rooted and built up in him, strengthened in the faith as you were taught, and overflowing with thankfulness. See to it that no one takes you captive through hollow and deceptive philosophy, which depends on human tradition and the basic principles of this world rather than on Christ.

—Colossians 2:6–8

But solid food is for the mature, who by constant use have trained themselves to distinguish good from evil.

—Hebrews 5:14

How can we equip ourselves and our kids for survival in a disintegrating culture? With _____ firmly believed, clearly taught, and consistently lived out.

Because how I think determines _____

For as he thinks within himself, so he is.

—Proverbs 23:7 (NASB)

Because I am commanded to:

1. _____

Be diligent to present yourself approved to God as a workman who does not need to be ashamed, handling accurately the word of truth.

—2 Timothy 2:15 (NASB)

Knowing the truth enables you to better *use* the truth.

2. _____

Teach me to live according to your truth, for you are my God, who saves me.

I always trust in you.

—Psalm 25:5 (GNT)

I have been sent to bring faith to those God has chosen and to teach them to know the truth that shows them how to live godly lives.

—Titus 1:1 (NLT)

3. _____

Sanctify Christ as Lord in your hearts, always being ready to make a defense to everyone who asks you to give an account for the hope that is in you, yet with gentleness and reverence.

—1 Peter 3:15 (NASB)

Warning: Knowledge all by itself can be very dangerous!

• Knowledge must be balanced with _____.

And this is my prayer: that your love may abound more and more in knowledge and depth of insight, so that you may be able to discern what is best.

—Philippians 1:9–10

Warning signs of knowledge without discernment: Knowledge remains theoretical; one person or group becomes a person's exclusive source of knowledge.

• Knowledge must be balanced with _____.

But grow in the grace and knowledge of our Lord and Savior Jesus Christ.

—2 Peter 3:18

Warning signs of knowledge without grace: Learning more about God without growing closer to God; legalism.

• Knowledge must be balanced with _____.

If I . . . can fathom all mysteries and all knowledge . . . but have not love, I am nothing.

—1 Corinthians 13:2

Knowledge puffs up, but love builds up.

—1 Corinthians 8:1

Warning signs of knowledge without love: Knowledge leads to intolerance of others; growth in knowledge leads to a growth in pride.

Building a Foundation That Lasts

Three Levels of Truth

Here's a brief look at what we'll be studying together. This chart helps you to see the different levels of learning that go along with grasping a truth. Being able to quote a truth does not mean I've fully grasped that truth.

To grasp a doctrine I must . . .	Learn It (understand the truth)	Love It (change my perspective)	Live It (apply it to life)
The Bible	The Bible is God's perfect guidebook for living.	I can make the right decision.	I will consult the Bible for guidance in my decision about _____.
God	God is bigger and better and closer than I can imagine.	The most important thing about me is what I believe about God.	When I see how great God is, it makes _____ look small.
Jesus	Jesus is God showing himself to us.	God wants me to know him better.	I will get to know Jesus through a daily quiet time.
The Holy Spirit	God lives in me and through me now.	I am a temple of God's Holy Spirit.	I will treat my body like the temple it is by _____.
Creation	Nothing "just happened." God created it all.	I have a purpose in this world.	The reason I exist is to _____.
Salvation	Grace is the only way to have a relationship with God.	I am an object of God's grace.	I'll stop seeing _____ as a way to earn my salvation. I'll begin doing it simply in appreciation for God's grace.
Sanctification	Faith is the only way to grow as a believer.	I grow when I see myself in a new way.	I'll spend more time listening to what God's Word says about me and less time listening to what the world says about me.
Good and Evil	God has allowed evil to provide us with a choice. God can bring good even out of evil events. God promises victory over evil to those who choose him.	All things work together for good.	I am battling evil as I face _____. I will overcome evil with good by _____.
The Afterlife	Heaven and hell are real places. Death is a beginning, not the end.	I can face death with confidence.	I will have a more hopeful attitude toward _____.
The Church	The only true "world superpower" is the church.	The best place to invest my life is in God's church.	I need to make a deeper commitment to the church by _____.
The Second Coming	Jesus is coming again to judge this world and to gather God's children.	I want to be living alertly for him when he comes.	Someone I can encourage with the hope of the Second Coming is _____.

Discussion Questions

1. Since this is your first time together as a group, take a few minutes to get to know each other. Share your name, where you were born, and one reason you decided to participate in this study.

2. When did understanding the truth about the Bible first become important to you? Tell about a time when knowing a truth was a real lifesaver. How has a truth about God and faith
   • helped you to deepen your relationship with God?
   • kept you from making a terrible mistake?
   • made you better able to serve God and others?
   • encouraged you in a time of trouble or temptation?
   • given you a new sense of freedom in your life?

3. If doctrine is so important, why do you think so many people seem to have a negative attitude toward the teaching of doctrine? Why do people so often see doctrine as something dry and boring, or loud and dogmatic?

4. Discuss things you can do to make sure your knowledge does not get out of balance. Don't just talk about what others should do; talk about what *you can* do. List two or three specific things that will help you and your group keep your knowledge balanced with love and grace and discernment.

Answers to Fill-Ins

organized summary

Bible teaches

faith seeking understanding

know God better

essential foundation

circumstances

false teachings

truth

how I act

study the truth

live the truth

defend the truth

discernment

grace

love

The Bible
Part 1

Life Change Objective

To deepen (or to form) your conviction that the Bible, as God's Word, can be trusted more than your feelings, values, opinions, and culture.

Three Important Words, Their Definitions, and Their Implications

Revelation

Revelation means that God has chosen to reveal his nature and his will to us through the Bible. The Bible was written so that God could show us what he is like and what he wants us to be like. An understanding of God comes solely through his decision to reveal himself to us.

> And so I will show my greatness and my holiness, and I will make myself known in the sight of many nations. Then they will know that I am the LORD.
>
> —Ezekiel 38:23

Inspiration

Inspiration is the process through which God gave us the Bible. God worked in the hearts of human writers to inspire them to write down his words. God's words written through these people are perfect, infallible, and trustworthy.

> All Scripture is inspired by God and is useful to teach us what is true and to make us realize what is wrong in our lives. It straightens us out and teaches us to do what is right.
>
> —2 Timothy 3:16 (NLT)

Illumination

Illumination is the Holy Spirit's work of bringing light to the words of the Bible as we read them. Illumination is the means by which we understand the Bible.

> Then he opened their minds so they could understand the Scriptures.
> —Luke 24:45

In the next study we'll focus on illumination. Now we'll look at three important questions related to the revelation and inspiration of God's Word.

How Do We Know the Bible Came from God?

First: The external evidence says the Bible is a historical book.

- The number of manuscript copies and the short length of time between the original manuscripts and our first copies of the New Testament

For the New Testament the evidence is overwhelming. There are 5,366 manuscripts to compare and draw information from, and some of these date from the second or third centuries. To put that in perspective, there are only 643 copies of Homer's *Iliad*, and that is the most famous book of ancient Greece! No one doubts the existence of Julius Caesar's *Gallic Wars*, but we only have 10 copies of it and the earliest of those was made 1,000 years after it was written. To have such an abundance of copies of the New Testament from dates within 70 years after their writing is amazing.[1]

—Norman Geisler

Why didn't God allow us to have the original rather than relying on a number of copies? One possibility: we would have worshiped an old document rather than reading and following his living Word.

- The extreme care with which the Scriptures were copied

- Confirmation of places and dates by archaeology

Discovery after discovery has established the accuracy of innumerable details, and has brought increased recognition to the value of the Bible as a source of history.[2]

—William F. Albright

Second: The internal evidence says the Bible is a unique book.

- The majority of the Bible is from eyewitness accounts.

- The amazing agreement and consistency throughout the Bible

The Bible was written over a period of about 1,500 years in various places stretching all the way from Babylon to Rome. The human authors included over 40 persons from various stations of life: kings, peasants, poets, herdsmen, fishermen, scientists, farmers, priests, pastors, tentmakers and governors. It was written in a wilderness, a dungeon, inside palaces and prisons, on lonely islands and in military battles. Yet it speaks with agreement and reliability on hundreds of controversial subjects. Yet it tells one story from beginning to end, God's salvation of man through Jesus Christ. NO PERSON could have possibly conceived of or written such a work![3]

—Josh McDowell

 ## A Closer Look

What's the Difference?

The Bible is translated from 24,000 copies of the New Testament alone, with millions of people having seen some of these copies. Those copies have been translated by thousands of scholars.	The Book of Mormon is translated from a supposed single original that is claimed to have been seen and translated by one man: Joseph Smith (who was not an expert in languages). That original was "taken back." There are no copies of that original.
The Bible was written by more than forty different authors spanning over fifty generations and three continents. It speaks with agreement on all matters of faith and doctrine.	The Qu'ran is the writings and record of one man, Muhammad, in one place at one point in history. It differs at many points with the Old and New Testament accounts of history.
The Bible provides God's distinctive solution to man's problem with sin and focuses on God's work in actual, verifiable history.	Hindu scriptures claim all roads lead to the same place and focus on stories of things that happened in the "celestial realms."

Third: The personal evidence says the Bible is a powerful book.

The Bible is the world's best-selling book. Most people know that it was the first major book to be printed on a press (the Gutenburg Bible). The Bible, in whole or in part, has been translated into more than 1,300 languages.

Millions of lives have been changed through the truth in the Bible!

Remember, personal testimony is just one of the four proofs that the Bible is God's book.

Fourth: _____ ***said the Bible came from God.***

1. Jesus recognized the Spirit as the _____.

   "Why, then," Jesus asked, "did the Spirit inspire David to call him 'Lord'? David said, 'The Lord said to my Lord: "Sit here at my right side until I put your enemies under your feet."'"

   —Matthew 22:43–44 (GNT)

2. Jesus quoted the Bible as _____.

   Jesus replied, "You are in error because you do not know the Scriptures or the power of God."

   —Matthew 22:29

   He replied, "Blessed rather are those who hear the word of God and obey it."

   —Luke 11:28

3. Jesus proclaimed its uniqueness.

   I tell you the truth, until heaven and earth disappear, not the smallest letter, not the least stroke of a pen, will by any means disappear from the Law until everything is accomplished.

   —Matthew 5:18

   Scripture is always true.

   —John 10:35 (NCV)

4. Jesus called it the "_____."

   Thus you nullify the word of God by your tradition that you have handed down. And you do many things like that.

   —Mark 7:13

5. Jesus believed that people and places in the Bible were real.

   - He believed in the _____ (Matt. 22:40; 24:15).

   - He believed in _____ (Luke 17:26).

   - He believed in _____ and _____ (Matt. 19:4).

   - He believed in _____ and _____ (Matt. 10:15).

   - He believed in _____ (Matt. 12:40).

How Do We Know We Have the Right Books?

The testimony of the _____

- Jesus recognized the Old Testament canon. The word *canon* refers to the list of books that are accepted as Scripture.

This is what I told you while I was still with you: Everything must be fulfilled that is written about me in the Law of Moses, the Prophets and the Psalms.

—Luke 24:44

- Peter recognized part of the New Testament canon.

  Some things in Paul's letters are hard to understand, and people who are ignorant and weak in faith explain these things falsely. They also falsely explain the other Scriptures, but they are destroying themselves by doing this.

  —2 Peter 3:16 (NCV)

- Paul recognized the _____ inspiration of the Old and New Testaments in a single verse.

  For the Scripture says, "Do not muzzle the ox while it is treading out the grain," and "The worker deserves his wages."

  —1 Timothy 5:18

This is an amazing verse. In it Paul quotes from Deuteronomy 25:4 in the Old Testament and from Luke 10:7 in the New Testament, and calls them both Scripture!

The history of the church

Books were included in the New Testament on the basis of three things:

1. The authority of an _____

   The New Testament has eyewitness authority. Take the writers of the Gospels, for instance. Matthew was an apostle, Mark wrote down Peter's remembrances, Luke was a friend of Paul, and John was an apostle.

2. The teaching of the _____

3. The confirmation of the _____

   Many people think that the New Testament books were chosen by a council of a few people. That is not true. A council did recognize the books of the New Testament (around 400 A.D.), but that was after the church had been using these books for 300 years. The council formally recognized the books in response to false teachers who were trying to add books to the Bible.

The power of God

The grass withers and the flowers fall, but the word of our God stands forever.

—Isaiah 40:8

Our assurance that we have the right books is a matter of _____. God would not have allowed any part of what he had chosen to stand forever to be left out.

What Does It Mean When We Say the Bible Is Inspired?

A Fresh Word

Inspiration

Inspiration does not mean simply that the writer felt enthusiastic, like Handel composing "The Messiah." Nor does it mean that the writings are necessarily inspiring, like an uplifting poem. As a process, it refers to the writers and the writings being controlled by God. As a product, it refers to the writings only, as documents that are God's message.[4]

—Norman Geisler

Inspiration means God wrote the Bible through

_____.

No prophecy ever came from what a person wanted to say, but people led by the Holy Spirit spoke words from God.

—2 Peter 1:21 (NCV)

Inspiration means the Holy Spirit is the _____.

The Scripture had to be fulfilled which the Holy Spirit spoke long ago through the mouth of David . . .

—Acts 1:16

The Holy Spirit spoke the truth to your forefathers when he said through Isaiah the prophet . . .

—Acts 28:25

Then the Spirit of the LORD came upon me, and he told me to say . . .

—Ezekiel 11:5

Two important words to understand:

Verbal: God inspired the _____, not just the ideas (Matt. 5:18; 22:43–44—Jesus based his argument on the single word "Lord").

Plenary: God inspired _____, not just part (2 Tim. 3:16).

As for God, his way is perfect; the word of the LORD is flawless. He is a shield for all who take refuge in him.

—Psalm 18:30

If you believe what you like in the Gospel, and reject what you don't like, it is not the Gospel you believe, but yourself.

—Augustine

***Inspiration means God's Word
is to be our*** _____.

> How can a young person stay pure? By obeying your word and following its rules.
>
> —Psalm 119:9 (NLT)

> For the word of the LORD holds true, and everything he does is worthy of our trust.
>
> —Psalm 33:4 (NLT)

- Understanding inspiration increases my _____ in the Bible.

- The truth behind inspiration is that I can trust his Word above my _____, _____, _____, and _____.

Whenever there is a conflict between what the Bible says and the way I feel or what I've been taught or the opinions of others or what seems reasonable to me—whenever I have a difference of opinion with the Bible for any reason—the Bible is always right!

Acting on the Truth

How Should We Respond?

The Bible shows us God. How should we respond to this book?
- With awe (Ps. 119:120)
- With delight (Ps. 1:2)
- With appreciation (Ps. 119:72)
- With praise (Ps. 119:62)
- With joy (Ps. 119:111)
- With love (Ps. 119:47, 97)
- With obedience (Deut. 5:32; James 1:22; John 14:15)

Use the verses above in your quiet time before the next session. Take a few moments not only to read the verse but also to do what it says. It's amazing how our faith in God's Word is increased through this simple step of telling God how we value his Word.

> **Begin working on *Foundations* memory card 1,
> "The Truth about the Bible."**

Discussion Questions

1. Take a moment to get to know each other better by filling in some of the following details of your personal histories.

   My Life Story

   Place I was born:

   Favorite subject in high school:

   One of my favorite TV shows growing up:

   The model and year of the first car I owned:

   My first job:

   My favorite candy bar as a kid:

2. Do you have a favorite verse or passage or book in the Bible? What is it and why?

3. Tell about a time when the Bible had an impact on your life.

4. What difference does it make whether the Gospels—or the other books of the Bible—are historically reliable?

5. In your reading of the Bible, what evidence have you seen that the Bible is both amazing and unique?

6. Give some examples of the struggle to

   trust God's Word above your feelings.

   trust God's Word above the values you've grown up with.

   trust God's Word above your opinions.

   trust God's Word above your culture.

7. How has this study helped you to see that trusting in the Bible as God's Word is more than just a feeling we have? What truths that we have looked at are the most convincing to you of the wonder and reliability of the Bible?

Answers to Fill-Ins

Jesus	apostle
author	truth
authoritative	church
Word of God	faith
prophets	people
Noah	author
Adam, Eve	words
Sodom, Gomorrah	all
Jonah	final authority
Bible	confidence
equal	feelings, values, opinions, culture

The Bible
Part 2

Life Change Objective

To give you deep and lasting confidence in your God-given ability to understand the Bible.

Remember the three words: revelation, inspiration, illumination?

- Revelation has been completed (Heb. 1:1–2).

- Inspiration has been completed (1 Peter 1:10–12).

- Illumination is going on right now.

> LORD, you have brought light to my life; my God, you light up my darkness.
>
> —Psalm 18:28 (NLT)

> Your word is a lamp to my feet and a light for my path.
>
> —Psalm 119:105

A Fresh Word

Illumination

Illumination is the supernatural influence or ministry of the Holy Spirit, which enables all who believe in Christ to understand the Scriptures.

Picture it this way: with his revelation and by his inspiration, God sent the light of his Word into our world. Through illumination, the blinders are taken off our eyes so that we can see the light that is already there.

Four things are necessary for illumination in a believer's life:

Love God's Word _____

> How I love your teachings! I think about them all day long.
>
> —Psalm 119:97 (NCV)

> Truly, I love your commands more than gold, even the finest gold.
>
> —Psalm 119:127 (NLT)

> And if you call out for insight and cry aloud for understanding, and if you look for it as for silver and search for it as for hidden treasure, then you will understand the fear of the LORD and find the knowledge of God. For the LORD gives wisdom, and from his mouth come knowledge and understanding.
>
> —Proverbs 2:3–6

How does the Bible picture its potential for changing our lives?

1. _____

> For you have been born again, not of perishable seed, but of imperishable, through the living and enduring word of God.
>
> —1 Peter 1:23

2. Sword

> Take the helmet of salvation and the sword of the Spirit, which is the word of God.
>
> —Ephesians 6:17

> For the word of God is living and active. Sharper than any double-edged sword, it penetrates even to dividing soul and spirit, joints and marrow; it judges the thoughts and attitudes of the heart.
>
> —Hebrews 4:12

In Ephesians the sword is in our hand, defending against the enemy. In Hebrews, the sword is in God's hands, penetrating and deeply impacting our lives.

3. _____

> When your words came, I ate them; they were my joy and my heart's delight, for I bear your name, O LORD God Almighty.
>
> —Jeremiah 15:16

> Jesus answered, "It is written: 'Man does not live on bread alone, but on every word that comes from the mouth of God.'"
>
> —Matthew 4:4

> Like newborn babies, crave pure spiritual milk, so that by it you may grow up in your salvation.
>
> —1 Peter 2:2

4. Fire and Hammer

"Is not my word like fire," declares the LORD, "and like a hammer that breaks a rock in pieces?"

—Jeremiah 23:29

5. Mirror

Anyone who listens to the word but does not do what it says is like a man who looks at his face in a mirror and, after looking at himself, goes away and immediately forgets what he looks like. But the man who looks intently into the perfect law that gives freedom, and continues to do this, not forgetting what he has heard, but doing it—he will be blessed in what he does.

—James 1:23–25

Understand God's Word _____

Two truths about every believer in Christ:

1. The Holy Spirit makes me _____ to understand the Bible.

And God has actually given us his Spirit (not the world's spirit) so we can know the wonderful things God has freely given us. When we tell you this, we do not use words of human wisdom. We speak words given to us by the Spirit, using the Spirit's words to explain spiritual truths. But people who aren't Christians can't understand these truths from God's Spirit. It all sounds foolish to them because only those who have the Spirit can understand what the Spirit means. We who have the Spirit understand these things, but others can't understand us at all.

—1 Corinthians 2:12–15 (NLT)

But when he, the Spirit of truth, comes, he will guide you into all truth.

—John 16:13

2. The Holy Spirit makes me _____ for understanding the Bible.

But you have an anointing from the Holy One, and all of you know the truth. . . . As for you, the anointing you received from him remains in you, and you do not need anyone to teach you. But as his anointing teaches you about all things and as that anointing is real, not counterfeit—just as it has taught you, remain in him.

—1 John 2:20, 27

Handle God's Word _____

Be diligent to present yourself approved to God as a workman who does not need to be ashamed, handling accurately the word of truth.

—2 Timothy 2:15 (NASB)

Seven rules of Bible study

Rule 1: Faith and the Holy Spirit are necessary for proper interpretation.

Rule 2: The Bible interprets itself.

Application: Learn to do cross-reference studies.

Rule 3: Understand the Old Testament in light of the

_____.

Example: The Old Testament Law

Rule 4: Understand unclear passages in the light of _____ passages.

Example: "Now if there is no resurrection, what will those do who are baptized for the dead?" (1 Cor. 15:29).

Rule 5: Understand words and verses in the light of their

_____.

Example: "Take life easy; eat, drink and be merry" (Luke 12:19).

Rule 6: Understand historical passages in the light of
_____ passages.

Examples:

"The king must not take many wives for himself, because they will lead him away from the Lord" (Deut. 17:17 NLT).

"Very early in the morning, while it was still dark, Jesus got up, left the house and went off to a solitary place, where he prayed" (Mark 1:35).

Rule 7: Understand personal experience in the light of Scripture.

Example: "Owe nothing to anyone" (Rom. 13:8 NASB).

Study God's Word _____

How do you decide to study God's Word as a lifetime commitment?

1. Vow before the Lord to trust in and commit to the truth of his Word.

Be diligent in these matters; give yourself wholly to them, so that everyone may see your progress. Watch your life and doctrine closely. Persevere in them.

—1 Timothy 4:15–16

2. Cultivate eagerness by examining God's Word for answers.

> They [the Bereans] received the message with great eagerness and examined the Scriptures every day to see if what Paul said was true.
>
> —Acts 17:11

3. Tell others what you're learning from God's Word.

> Let the word of Christ dwell in you richly as you teach and admonish one another with all wisdom.
>
> —Colossians 3:16

4. *Act* on what you learn as you study the Bible.

> Do not merely listen to the word, and so deceive yourselves. Do what it says.
>
> —James 1:22

> **Finish memorizing *Foundations* memory card 1,
> "The Truth about the Bible."**

Discussion Questions

1. Tell about an experience that caused you to feel that you really love the Bible. What kinds of experiences cause you to feel this way? When do you most deeply feel the truth that the Bible is a treasure?

2. Discuss together your answers to the following:

   The Bible was like a seed to me when . . .

   The Bible was like a sword to me when . . .

   The Bible was like food to me when . . .

   The Bible was like a hammer to me when . . .

   The Bible was like a fire to me when . . .

   The Bible was like a mirror to me when . . .

3. The Holy Spirit gives us understanding of God's Word individually. John says we don't "need anyone to teach us." Yet the New Testament talks about, and even tells us to honor, the gifts of teaching and preaching. Why do we need teachers? How do these two truths fit together?

4. Which of the seven rules of Bible study do you think Christians most often stretch or break? How can we remind ourselves to handle the Bible accurately?

For Further Study

Anders, Max. *The Bible*. Nashville: Nelson, 1995.

Elwell, Walter, ed. *Topical Analysis of the Bible*. Grand Rapids, Mich.: Baker, 1991.

Little, Paul. *Know What You Believe*. Wheaton, Ill.: Victor, 1987.

McDowell, Josh. *The New Evidence That Demands a Verdict*. Nashville: Nelson Reference, 1999.

Mears, Henrietta. *What the Bible Is All About*. Ventura, Calif.: Regal, 1997.

Rhodes, Ron. *The Heart of Christianity*. Eugene, Ore.: Harvest House, 1996.

Warren, Rick. *Personal Bible Study Methods*. Available at www.Pastors.com.

Answers to Fill-Ins

deeply	accurately
seed	New Testament
food	clear
spiritually	context
able	doctrinal
responsible	diligently

God
Part 1

Life Change Objectives

- To gain a deeper sense of God's love for you as a Father.

- To act in some new way on the fact that God is your Father.

> What comes into our minds when we think about God is the most important thing about us. [1]
>
> —A. W. Tozer

> If you can understand it, it's not God.
>
> —Augustine

As we look at God's existence, we need to remember three key truths:

1. God is real.
2. God is revealed.
3. God is relational.

God Is Real

God is not a character in a story, in some fairy tale. He is as real as we are.

How do we know God exists?

1. We see God's _____ in what he has made (Gen 1:1; Rom 1:19–20; Acts 14:16–17).

   The heavens declare the glory of God; the skies proclaim the work of his hands. Day after day they pour forth speech; night after night they display knowledge.

   —Psalm 19:1–2

2. We see God's _____ on human history.

From one man he made every nation of men, that they should inhabit the whole earth; and he determined the times set for them and the exact places where they should live. God did this so that men would seek him and perhaps reach out for him and find him, though he is not far from each one of us.

—Acts 17:26–27

3. We see God's _____ in our lives.

Look at the story of Elijah and his battle with the false prophets on Mount Carmel in 1 Kings 18:24–39.

A Closer Look

What Does God Look Like?

The Bible tells us that no one has actually seen God (John 1:18). God is spirit (Ps. 139:7–12; John 4:24); God is invisible (John 1:18; Col. 1:15; Heb. 11:27). The natural assumption, when hearing the phrase that we are all "made in his image," is to think that God must look something like us: with two arms and two legs. What a scary thought! God, who fills this universe, obviously couldn't look like a man. When the Bible speaks of God having "strong arms" or "sheltering wings," these are not literal descriptions but pictures of how God relates to us.

God Is Revealed

God is not discovered by us, he _____ to us (Gen. 35:7; Ps. 98:2).

1. God reveals himself to us through _____.

From the time the world was created, people have seen the earth and sky and all that God made. They can clearly see his invisible qualities—his eternal power and divine nature. So they have no excuse whatsoever for not knowing God.

—Romans 1:20 (NLT)

2. God reveals himself to us through _____.

Above all, you must understand that no prophecy in Scripture ever came from the prophets themselves or because they wanted to prophesy. It was the Holy Spirit who moved the prophets to speak from God.

—2 Peter 1:20–21 (NLT)

3. God reveals himself to us through _____.

No one has seen God at any time; the only begotten God, who is in the bosom of the Father, He has explained Him.

—John 1:18 (NASB)

Jesus came to give us understanding (1 John 5:20). Jesus chose to reveal the Father to us (Matt. 11:27). God has revealed himself in many ways, but his last word and clearest revelation is in Jesus (Heb. 1:1–2).

Gallup surveys consistently show 96 percent of Americans believe that God is real. For most people, whether God exists is not the issue. The real issue is, What kind of a God is he? What does Jesus reveal to us about God?

God Is Relational

Let's look at some popular ideas about what kind of a God lives in heaven and see what the Bible has to say about the real God.

The truth about God

The popular idea is: God is distant.

The truth is: God is _____ (Ps. 139:7–12; James 4:8).

The popular idea is: God watches our actions from afar.

The truth is: God is intimately involved in _____ _____ of our lives (Matt. 6:25–30; Luke 12:6–7).

The popular idea is: God is anxiously waiting to judge those who do wrong.

The truth is: God is waiting to _____ all who ask (John 3:17).

The popular idea is: God is either powerless against or doesn't care about much of the evil in the world.

The truth is: God allows an evil world to continue to exist so that more people might be saved out of it (2 Peter 3:8–9).

A Fresh Word

Four theological words provide the background for the statements we've covered about the real person of God:

1. God's immanence: God is awesomely near to all of us. God is not beyond the farthest star; he is as near as our next heartbeat. He does not just watch us; he is with us.

2. God's omnipresence: God is everywhere (omni = all + present). His presence fills the universe. He is everyplace all at once.

3. God's omniscience: God knows everything (omni = all + scient = knowing). He knows everything that has happened, is happening, and will happen. He knows what I will think before I think it.

4. God's omnipotence: God is all mighty (omni = all + potent). He has the power to do anything—*anything*—he wants. Immediately!

To sum it up:
In a world in which people see God as _____,
the truth is that God is _____.

The number 1 way we see that God is relational

Jesus taught us to call God our _____.

God relates to us as a perfect Father:

1. Our Father is willing to make _____. He sent his Son into the world to die as our Savior (John 3:16; 1 John 4:14).

2. Our Father has _____ and love for his children (Ps. 103:13; 2 Cor. 1:3).

3. Our Father _____ his children (Prov. 3:12).

4. Our Father knows our needs before we ask (Matt. 6:8; 7:9–11); that's why we pray "Our Father" (Matt. 6:9).

5. Our Father _____ us (Matt. 6:20; Heb. 11:6).

6. Our Father makes us his heirs (Rom. 8:15–17).

7. Our Father _____ us (2 Thess. 2:16–17).

8. Our Father shows no _____ among his children.

- He gives access to all equally (Eph. 2:18).

- He blesses all richly (Rom. 10:12).

- He judges each person impartially (1 Peter 1:17).

Jesus told us: "Anyone who has seen _____ has seen the Father" (John 14:9).

Key Personal Perspective

You may be having a hard time thinking of God as a Father because of the poor father you had growing up. One of the most refreshing breakthroughs in your life will happen when you begin to see God as the Father you never had, to see God as the Father who fulfills what your father never was.

Start or strengthen this new perspective in your life by praying the following prayer. (Pray those parts that are appropriate for your life and add to the prayer where you need to.)

God, I now accept you as the Father I never had. I was disappointed by my father, but you will never disappoint me. I never knew my earthly father, but you want to know me. I was hurt by my earthly father, but I am healed by you. I was ignored by my earthly father, but I have your full and constant attention. I could never meet the expectations of my earthly father, but I can find freedom from expectations in your grace. Amen.

Maybe you had an earthly father who, although he was not perfect, gave you the kind of love that put you on the road to finding a relationship with God through Jesus. You need to pray,

Thank you, God, for my earthly father. I know he wasn't perfect in the way he raised me, but he was good and he was kind and he was a man of character. He made decisions in his life that helped me to see a little bit of what you are like, decisions that made it easier for me to get to know you. Thank you for the gift he gave me. Amen.

Acting on the Truth

Truth can seem cold and distant until we see how it fits into our lives. How does the truth of God's reality fit you in a personal way? Worship!

1. Before the next session, read the following passages of Scripture, in which God speaks about his reality. As you read, focus on listening to God. Hear him speaking directly and personally to you.

   "You are my witnesses," declares the LORD, "and my servant whom I have chosen, so that you may know and believe me and understand that I am he. Before me no god was formed, nor will there be one after me."

   —Isaiah 43:10

   See now that I myself am He! There is no god besides me. I put to death and I bring to life, I have wounded and I will heal.

   —Deuteronomy 32:39

   This is what the LORD says—Israel's King and Redeemer, the LORD Almighty: I am the first and I am the last; apart from me there is no God. . . . Do not tremble, do not be afraid. Did I not proclaim this and foretell it long ago? You are my witnesses. Is there any God besides me? No, there is no other Rock; I know not one.

   —Isaiah 44:6, 8

2. Concentrate on God's power and control as you remember some of the significant things he has done in your life.

   You don't have to be a history major to see God's work in human history. Think about the fact that all of history is divided by the life of Christ. Consider how history has shown us that the most powerful of human governments rise and fall. Get out a piece of paper and use it to finish the sentence, "God, I see your control over human history when I look at . . ."

   Now finish the sentence, "God, I see your control over my life when I look at . . ."

3. Consider God's beauty and creativity as you close your eyes and think about something he has made. Better yet, get out there and see it!

4. Jesus taught us to call God "Abba." The word *Abba* is the intimate name for a father that a little child would use, like our word *Daddy*. In your prayers this week, try addressing God as Abba or even Daddy. (Don't think of it as irreverent; it's a word that expresses your intimate connection with and your ultimate dependence on God.)

5. It helps some people to picture being in the presence of God. We don't worship the picture; it simply helps us to worship God. Picture God as your Father. Picture him walking up to you, taking your face tenderly in his hands, and asking you, "What do you want me to do for you today?"[2]

Begin working on memory card 2, "The Truth about God."

Discussion Questions

1. When you think of God, do you have a picture in your mind? What is that picture?

2. What is the one thing that for you makes it seem as if God is in the room with you? What makes God seem the most real to you? Seeing what he has made? Being in church? Reading the Bible? Looking at human history?

3. Look at the list of popular ideas about God and the truths about God. In this list, which popular idea do you think is potentially the most damaging? Which truth is the most difficult for you to accept (perhaps because of the teaching or the culture you were brought up in)?

4. Is there any part of this study that wasn't made as clear to you as you would like? What question that you had about what we discussed was not answered?

5. What is it about God's love that most helps you to see him as a perfect Father? How has God shown his love as a Father to you? For ideas, review the list we covered of eight ways God meets our needs by relating to us as a Father.

Answers to Fill-Ins

creativity	unapproachable
thumbprint	relational
actions	Father
reveals himself	sacrifices
his creation	compassion
his Word	guides
his Son	rewards
near	encourages
every detail	favoritism
forgive	me

God
Part 2

Life Change Objective

To develop a sense of amazement about God that results in a decision to spend time getting to know him.

In this study, we're going to focus on three characteristics unique to the person of God.

We looked in the last study at the clearest expression of the truth that God is personal: the fact that he is our Father. We are going to focus today on three additional aspects of God's person that we all need to know and understand. If God took a personality test, he would not be described with terms as limited as "sanguine," "dominant," or "introspective." The following three characteristics are unique to the person of God.

God Exists as a _____

A Fresh Word

Trinity

God is three in one—Father, Son, and Holy Spirit. He is not three Gods, nor is he one God acting in three different ways. The Bible tells us that God is three different and distinct persons, and that these three different and distinct persons are one in the being of God.

Pictures and statements regarding the Trinity

The doctrine of the Trinity is not found in any single verse of the Bible. It is to be found in a study of the whole of the Bible.

St. Patrick's picture of the Trinity was the three-leafed shamrock.

Some use the picture of the three forms of water: ice, liquid, and steam. Water under pressure and in a vacuum at a given temperature below freezing exists simultaneously as ice, liquid, and gas; yet it is identifiable always as water (H_2O), its basic nature. In physics this is called "the triple point of water."

Others use a much simpler picture: Neapolitan ice cream! The three flavors are distinct and separate, yet without any one of them it would not be Neapolitan.

> When I first began to study the Bible years ago, the doctrine of the Trinity was one of the most complex problems I had to encounter. I have never fully resolved it, for it contains an aspect of mystery. Though I do not totally understand it to this day, I accept it as a revelation of God.[1]
>
> —Billy Graham

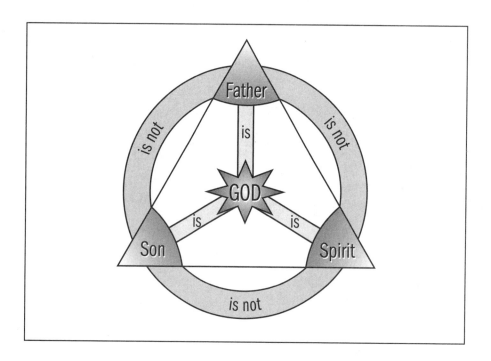

The truth of the Trinity is shown by the Bible's teaching that . . .

1. God is _____.

   The LORD our God, the LORD is one.

   —Deuteronomy 6:4

   I am God, and there is no other; I am God, and there is none like me.

   —Isaiah 46:9

2. Father, Son, and Spirit are all called God.

   • The Father is God.

   Grace and peace to you from God our Father and from the Lord Jesus Christ.

   —Romans 1:7

   • Jesus is God.

Thomas said to him, "My Lord and my God!"

—John 20:28

In the beginning the Word already existed. He was with God, and he was God.

—John 1:1 (NLT)

- The Spirit is God.

    And I will ask the Father, and he will give you another Counselor to be with you forever—the Spirit of truth. The world cannot accept him, because it neither sees him nor knows him. But you know him, for he lives with you and will be in you.

    —John 14:16–17

    Ananias, how is it that Satan has so filled your heart that you have lied to the Holy Spirit. . . . You have not lied to men but to God.

    —Acts 5:3–4

3. Father, Son, and Spirit are _____ from one another.

    Jesus is distinct from the Father. (He prayed to the Father in John 17.)

    The Spirit is distinct from the Father (John 14:26).

    The Son is distinct from the Spirit (John 14:16–17).

The conclusion is: God is one in being, but he exists in three persons.

Glimpses of the Trinity

- God speaks of himself as "_____" in four places in the Old Testament (Gen. 1:26; 3:22; 11:7; Isa. 6:8).

- All three persons were involved in Creation (the Spirit—Gen. 1:2; the Father—Heb. 1:2; the Son—Col. 1:15–16).

- We are _____ in the name of the Father, the Son, and the Spirit (Matt. 28:19).

- All three persons were at Jesus' _____ (Mark 1:10–11) and in Jesus' _____ (Luke 1:35).

- The Bible tells us all three persons were the power behind Jesus' _____. In John 2:19, Jesus said he would raise his body. In Romans 8:11 we're told that the Holy Spirit raised Jesus. In Acts 3:26, the Father raised the Son. This makes sense only when you understand the truth of the Trinity. Only God can raise someone from the dead.

- Paul's prayer in 2 Corinthians 13:14: "the grace of the Lord Jesus Christ, and the love of God, and the fellowship of the Holy Spirit."

- Jesus' promise to his disciples in John 14:16–17: Jesus says he will ask the Father for the Spirit.

Key Personal Perspective

Why Is This Important?

Theologically: Understanding the truth of the Trinity prevents us from adopting inadequate views of God.

It prevents us from seeing Jesus and the Spirit as less than God; from seeing Jesus and the Father as exactly the same; and from thinking that there are three gods rather than just one.

One of our inevitable temptations as human beings is to see God as less than who he is. The truth of the Trinity helps us to resist this temptation.

Personally: The Trinity is a reminder of the majesty and mystery of the God who gave himself for us on the cross.

You trust the truth of the Trinity:

- When you ask for salvation (the Spirit convicts—John 16:8; the Son sacrifices—Heb. 10:10; the Father gives—John 3:16).
- Every time you pray (the Spirit communicates—Rom. 8:26; Jesus intercedes—Rom. 8:34; the Father answers—John 16:23–24).

Relationally: The Trinity shows us that God in his very essence is relational.

Even before he created us, there was a perfect relationship between God the Father, God the Son, and God the Spirit. God did not need to create us in order to have someone to relate to, because he already had the perfect relationship in the Trinity. Our ability to relate to one another and to enjoy our relationship with God grows out of his relational nature.

God Is Absolutely _____

Sovereignty refers not to God's attitude but to the reality of who he is. God is not someone with a dominating personality; he is a person who is absolutely dominant. God is not controlling; he is in ultimate control. God does not need to take charge because he always is in charge.

1. He is greater than and exists above his creation: he is

   _____.

   > But will God really dwell on earth? The heavens, even the highest heaven, cannot contain you. How much less this temple I have built!
   > —1 Kings 8:27

   > One God and Father of all, who is over all and through all and in all.
   > —Ephesians 4:6

   - He is greater than time (Isa. 57:15; Deut. 33:27; Ps. 90:2).

   - He is greater than place (Ps. 139:7–10; Jer. 23:23; Acts 17:24–28).

   - He is greater than circumstance (James 1:17; 1 Sam. 15:29; Mal. 3:6).

   Nothing _____ God (Ps. 139:2–4).

2. He never needs permission or help: he is

   _____.

   > And he is not served by human hands, as if he needed anything, because he himself gives all men life and breath and everything else.
   > —Acts 17:25

   > Who are you, a mere human being, to criticize God? Should the thing that was created say to the one who made it, "Why have you made me like this?"
   > —Romans 9:20 (NLT)

3. God can do anything he wants: he is _____.

   > He counts the stars and calls them all by name. How great is our Lord! His power is absolute! His understanding is beyond comprehension!
   > —Psalm 147:4–5 (NLT)

   Fifty-six times the Bible says that God is the Almighty One.

A Fresh Word

For just a moment, think again about the words we've been using to describe God. These words are often misunderstood. They have taken on meanings that make us feel that God is an impersonal God. This should be no surprise since one of Satan's schemes is to twist and degrade the name and person of God in order to lessen his impact in the world and in our lives. Satan is at the head of an evil PR campaign that seeks to defame the character of God. Here's the truth about some of the words we commonly use to describe God.

Holy does not mean God is picky or judgmental or "holier than thou." To be holy, literally, is to be separate and distinct. Holy means God has perfect integrity. In fact, he is the only being in the universe with perfect integrity.

Eternal does not mean that God is old or tired or out of date. God has always existed. He stands outside of time, able to see the entire history of the universe at a glance.

Transcendent does not mean that God cannot understand our needs and hurts. It does not mean, as in the Bette Midler song, that he's watching us "from a distance." The fact that God stands above and beyond his creation does not mean he stands outside his creation. He is both transcendent (above and beyond his creation) and immanent (within and throughout his creation).

Almighty does not mean that God does whatever he wants with no thought to the impact on us. He uses his power to create and to love his creation.

All-knowing does not mean that God is some kind of cosmic Big Brother, watching and judging us but never really caring about us. We know that as human beings we could not see all of the pain in the world without somehow becoming numb to it, but God is not like that. He can see all that happens and still deeply care about everything that happens.

God Is _____

"God is good, all the time.

"All the time, God is good."

- He acts in _____ (Lev. 11:44; Isa. 6:1–3).

  In the year that King Uzziah died, I saw the Lord seated on a throne, high and exalted, and the train of his robe filled the temple. Above him were seraphs, each with six wings: With two wings they covered their faces, with two they covered their feet, and with two they were flying. And they were calling to one another:

  > "Holy, holy, holy is the LORD Almighty;
  > the whole earth is full of his glory."

  —Isaiah 6:1–3

- He relates in _____ (Ex. 34:6; Lam. 3:22; James 5:11).

- His _____ can be trusted (Ps. 36:5; Heb. 10:23).

- His _____ is unequaled (Ps. 34:8; 2 Peter 1:3).

- His _____ is impartial and fair (Isa. 30:18; Luke 18:7–8).

- He reacts to sin in _____ (Gen. 6:5–8; Rom. 2:5–9; 1 Thess. 2:16).

- He is _____ (1 John 4:7–11; John 3:16).

Key Personal Perspective

The Bible often talks about God's nature in terms of a personal challenge to us. We are created in his image (Gen. 1:27). What he is like in character is what we should become like. Some of God's attributes are his alone, such as omnipotence or eternalness, but we are to reflect others in our lives. How can that happen? A simple truth of human nature applies here: we become like those we spend the most time with. When I spend time with God, I inevitably become more like him.

His person empowers my character!

Finish memorizing memory card 2, "The Truth about God."
If you invest a little time each week memorizing these truths,
you'll increase your ability to apply them to your everyday life.
You'll also be able to share them more clearly with others.

Appendix

Theology of the Trinity

Introduction	The word *Trinity* is never used, nor is the doctrine of Trinitarianism ever explicitly taught, in the Scriptures, but Trinitarianism is the best explication [detailed explanation] of the biblical evidence. It is a crucial doctrine for Christianity because it focuses on who God is, and particularly on the deity of Jesus Christ. Because Trinitarianism is not taught explicitly in the Scriptures, the study of the doctrine is an exercise in putting together biblical themes and data through a systematic theological study and through looking at the historical development of the present orthodox view of what the biblical presentation of the Trinity is.	
Essential Elements of the Trinity	God is One. Each of the persons within the Godhead is Deity. The oneness of God and threeness of God are not contradictory. The Trinity (Father, Son, and Holy Spirit) is eternal. Each of the persons of God is of the same essence and is not inferior or superior to the others in essence. The Trinity is a mystery which we will never be able to understand fully.	
Biblical Teaching	Old Testament	New Testament
God Is One	"Hear, O Israel: The LORD our God, the LORD is one" (Deut. 6:4; cf. 20:2–4; 3:13–15).	"Now to the King eternal, immortal, invisible, the only God, be honor and glory for ever and ever. Amen" (1 Tim. 1:17; cf. 1 Cor. 8:4–6; 1 Tim. 2:5–6; James 2:19).
Three Distinct Persons as Deity	The Father: "He said to me, 'You are my Son; today I have become your Father'" (Ps. 2:7).	"... who have been chosen according to the foreknowledge of God the Father" (1 Peter 1:2; cf. John 1:17; 1 Cor. 8:6; Phil. 2:11).
	The Son: "He said to me, 'You are my Son; today I have become your Father'" (Ps. 2:7; cf. Heb. 1:1–13; Ps. 68:18; Isa. 6:1–3; 9:6).	"As soon as Jesus was baptized, he went up out of the water. At that moment heaven was opened, and he saw the Spirit of God descending like a dove and lighting on him. And a voice from heaven said, 'This is my Son, whom I love; with him I am well pleased'" (Matt. 3:16–17).
	The Holy Spirit: "In the beginning God created the heavens and the earth.... and the Spirit of God was hovering over the waters" (Gen. 1:1–2; cf. Ex. 31:3; Judg. 15:14; Isa. 11:2).	"Then Peter said, 'Ananias, how is it that Satan has so filled your heart that you have lied to the Holy Spirit ...? You have not lied to men but to God'" (Acts 5:3–4; cf. 2 Cor. 3:17).
Plurality of Persons in the Godhead	The use of plural pronouns points to, or at least suggests, the plurality of persons within the Godhead in the Old Testament. "Then God said, 'Let us make man in our image, in our likeness ...'" (Gen. 1:26).	The use of the singular word "name" when referring to God the Father, Son, and Holy Spirit indicates a unity within the threeness of God. "Therefore go and make disciples of all nations, baptizing them in the name of the Father and of the Son and of the Holy Spirit" (Matt. 28:19).

Appendix *cont.*

	Attribute	Father	Son	Holy Spirit
Persons of the Same Essence: Attributes Applied to Each Person	Eternality	Ps. 90:2	John 1:2; Rev. 1:8, 17	Heb. 9:14
	Power	1 Peter 1:5	2 Cor. 12:9	Rom. 15:19
	Omniscience	Jer. 17:10	Rev. 2:23	1 Cor. 2:11
	Omnipresence	Jer. 23:24	Matt. 18:20	Ps. 139:7
	Holiness	Rev. 15:4	Acts 3:14	Acts 1:8
	Truth	John 7:28	Rev. 3:7	1 John 5:6
	Benevolence	Rom. 2:4	Eph. 5:25	Neh. 9:20
Equality with Different Roles: Activities Involving	Creation of the World	Ps. 102:25	Col. 1:16	Job 33:4
	Creation of Man	Gen. 2:7	Col. 1:16	Gen. 1:2; Job 26:13
	Baptism of Christ	Matt. 3:17	Matt. 3:16–17	Matt. 3:16
	Death of Christ	Heb. 9:14	Heb. 9:14	Heb. 9:14

Source: Taken from *Charts of Christian Theology and Doctrine* by H. Wayne House. Copyright " 1992 by H. Wayne House. Used by permission of Zondervan.

Discussion Questions

1. Did you find yourself thinking more about God as your Father this week? Share the place or circumstance in which you were reminded that he is your Father.

2. Share what you experienced in the four worship exercises from the last study mentioned in the bullets below.

   - After reading through the passages of Scripture in which God speaks about his own reality, what truths hit you?

   - As you took some time to concentrate on God's power and control by remembering some of the significant things he has done in your life, what did you remember?

   - What did you write about how you can see God's hand in human history?

   - Share with the group your experiences as you took some time to consider God's beauty and creativity by thinking about or taking a closer look at his creation.

3. It's easy to react to the teaching of the Trinity with a feeling of, "Who cares . . . just so I know Jesus loves me." How has this study helped you see why the truth of the Trinity is important?

   • What false teachings about God does the truth of the Trinity combat?

   • How does (or how could) this truth help you personally?

4. How does the truth that God is greater than time or place or circumstance help you to deal with a specific situation you're facing right now?

5. As we come to the end of our look at the person of God,

   • What new thing did you learn about God?

   • What did you learn that made God seem a little closer, a little less distant?

   • What did you learn about God that made you smile, made you able to enjoy him more?

   • What did you learn about God that made you feel more loved by him?

   • What did you learn about God that helped you understand his greatness in a clearer way?

   • What did you learn about God that increased your desire to devote your life to him?

   • What did you learn about God that increased your sense of security in everyday life?

6. The ways that God acts toward us are an obvious guide for how he wants us to act toward others. While we cannot have many of the characteristics of God (none of us is all-powerful or perfect), all of us can develop more of the character of God (compassion, love, goodness, forgiveness) and display it to the world around us.

   God desires for his character to be shown in the world. One of the ways we express faith as believers is to pray that his character will be revealed through us in the world. Use the following questions to develop a prayer list that will be a part of your "group prayer list." One of the most exciting things that you will experience as a group is the way that God will answer many of the prayers you put on this list.

   • Where in this world (or in your world) would you most like to see people recognize God's compassion?

   • Who do you most hope could tie in to God's wisdom?

   • Who or what are you counting on God to be patient with?

   • What relationship would you like to see God make right?

(Be specific in your prayer requests. If your concern is for your sister, don't say "my family." Let the group in on the details of what you would like them to pray for.)

For Further Study

Elwell, Walter, ed. *Topical Analysis of the Bible*. Grand Rapids, Mich.: Baker, 1991.

Little, Paul. *Know What You Believe*. Wheaton, Ill.: Victor, 1987.

Packer, J. I. *Knowing God*. Downers Grove, Ill.: InterVarsity Press, 1973.

Rhodes, Ron. *The Heart of Christianity*. Eugene, Ore.: Harvest House, 1996.

Sproul, R. C. *The Character of God*. Ann Arbor: Vine, 1982.

Tozer, A. W. *The Pursuit of God*. Camp Hill, Penn.: Christian Publications, 1982.

Zacharias, Ravi. *Can Man Live without God?* Nashville: Word, 1994.

Answers to Fill-Ins

trinity

one

distinct

us

baptized

baptism

birth announcement

resurrection

sovereign

transcendent

surprises

all-sufficient

almighty

perfectly moral

holiness

compassion

faithfulness

goodness

justice

wrath

love

Jesus
Part 1

Life Change Objectives

- To enable you to get to know your best friend, Jesus Christ, better than you ever have before.

- To encourage you to act on the truth that Jesus is your best friend in one specific way.

The object of this study is simple: to get to know Jesus better. I want you to get to know your best friend, Jesus Christ. The teaching centers around getting to know Jesus as you would get to know anyone: by learning his names, by understanding his life history, and by appreciating and enjoying his personality.

Why Is This Important?

1. Knowing Jesus is life's continuing _____.

2. Knowing Jesus is the believer's continuing _____.

> For as you know him better, he will give you, through his great power, everything you need for living a truly good life: he even shares his own glory and his own goodness with us!
>
> —2 Peter 1:3 (LB)

The Names of Jesus

One of the first ways we get to know another person is by learning his name. That's not such a simple task when it comes to Jesus. Elwell's *Topical Analysis of the Bible* lists 184 different names for Christ in the Bible.[1]

Remember, a name helps you to identify someone. The names of Jesus Christ help you to identify who he is.

A Fresh Word

A Person's Name

In the Bible, names had more significance than we sometimes give them today. A name was an indicator of three specifics about a person:

1. His purpose   2. His position   3. His promise

- The angel told Mary: Jesus (Luke 1:31).

  Jesus means "salvation of God."

- The angels told the shepherds (Luke 2:11):

- Savior: Showing Jesus' _____.

- Christ: Showing Jesus' _____.

- Lord: Showing Jesus' _____.

Jesus Christ, today I want to begin a relationship with you. I don't want to just know about you; I want to know you personally. I ask you to forgive me for the wrong things I've done. I want to learn from you how to live. I choose today to begin to live by your direction and guidance. I don't even know all that that will mean, but I'm trusting you to show me the way. In Jesus' name, amen.

Key Personal Perspective

The Bible does more than just list Jesus' names; it tells us of the power of his name!

Certain names *do* have power. List below some of the names in our world today that have certain power or authority or clout behind them.

1. Jesus' name is above all names (Phil. 2:9–11).

   Therefore God exalted him to the highest place and gave him the name that is above every name, that at the name of Jesus every knee should bow, in heaven and on earth and under the earth, and every tongue confess that Jesus Christ is Lord, to the glory of God the Father.

   —Philippians 2:9–11

2. As believers we live in his name!

We are anointed (James 5:14),
forgiven (1 John 2:12),
baptized (Acts 10:48),
and justified in his name (1 Cor. 6:11).

We assemble in his name (1 Cor. 5:4),
we bear his name (1 Peter 4:16),
believe in his name (John 1:12),
and call on his name (1 Cor. 1:2).

In his name we give thanks (Eph. 5:20),
have life (John 20:31),
preach (Acts 8:12),
speak (Acts 9:28),
and suffer (Acts 21:13; 1 Peter 4:16).

We do everything in his name (Col. 3:17).

The Details of Jesus' Life

Jesus' life did not begin with his birth and it did not end with his death. We're going to look at Jesus' life before, during, and after his time on this earth. If you did a time line of Jesus' life, his time on earth would be an exclamation point in the middle of an eternally long line. We see it as the larger part, and it is the most significant part for us, but in terms of real time, it is the shortest part.

What did Jesus do before he was born?
The pre-incarnate Christ

• He has always existed: he is eternal (Mic. 5:2; John 8:57–58).

• He _____ the universe (Col. 1:16).

• He _____ to people.

The people Jesus ministered to included:

1. Hagar (Gen. 16:7–14):

> The angel of the LORD found Hagar near a spring in the desert....Then the angel of the LORD told her, "Go back to your mistress and submit to her." The angel added, "I will so increase your descendants that they will be too numerous to count."
>
> —Genesis 16:7, 9–10

2. Moses (Ex. 3:2–14):

> The angel of the LORD appeared to him in flames of fire from within a bush. . . . God called to him from within the bush, "Moses! Moses!"
>
> —Exodus 3:2, 4

3. Abraham (Gen. 18:1–2; 22:11–12):

> The LORD appeared to Abraham near the great trees of Mamre. . . . Abraham looked up and saw three men standing nearby.
>
> —Genesis 18:1–2

A Fresh Word

The Angel of the Lord

A number of times in the Old Testament a figure called "the angel of the Lord" appears to people. It is evident that this is more than an angel. He is spoken of in terms that relate more to God himself. There is no single biblical reference regarding the identity of the angel of the Lord, but the great majority of Bible teachers see these as appearances of Christ on earth before his human birth. No, he did not look like Jesus of Nazareth. He did not become a man as he would when he was born in Bethlehem. He simply took on the appearance of a man.

In Genesis 16 the angel whom Hagar saw said that he would increase her descendants; only God would say that. And Hagar recognizes this angel as "the God who sees me." The Bible itself refers to him as "the LORD who spoke to her."

In Exodus 3 we are told, "The angel of the LORD appeared to him in flames of fire from within a bush. . . . God called to him from within the bush, 'Moses! Moses!'" (Ex. 3:2, 4). And Genesis 18:1–2 tells us that the Lord appeared to Abraham, also in the form of a man.

Jesus' life on earth
A short history

Although Jesus is eternal, we are most acquainted with the thirty-three short years that he walked this earth. One part of making friends with someone is getting to know the facts about him: where he was born, important relationships, memorable events, and so on. How do the stories you've heard about the life of Jesus fit into the overall history of his life? As we see the events of Jesus' earthly life, we have an opportunity to get to know him better.

A look at Jesus' life in six major periods

1. Jesus' _____

   Beginning: his birth (Matt. 1–2; Luke 1:1–2:38)

   Ending: Jesus in the temple (Luke 2:41–50)

   Significant Events:

   Jesus' dedication at the temple (Luke 2:22–39)

   Fleeing to Egypt (Matt. 2:13–23)

   Visit to the temple at age twelve (Luke 2:41–50)

"The Silent Years" of Jesus' Life

- Jesus grew as any child should grow.

  And Jesus grew in wisdom and stature, and in favor with God and men.

  —Luke 2:52

- His mother, Mary, was with him at his birth (of course! Luke 2:7), at his death (John 19:25), to witness his resurrection, and for the beginning of the church on the day of Pentecost (Acts 1:14; 2:1).

- His father, Joseph, probably died sometime after Jesus' visit to the temple in Jerusalem and before the beginning of his public ministry at age thirty. Joseph is never mentioned after the experience in the temple, although Mary is with Jesus numerous times. It would have been very unusual in that day for Mary to be traveling without her husband if he were still alive.

- There were at least seven children in Jesus' family: Jesus, four half brothers, and at least two half sisters (half brothers and half sisters because God was the Father of Jesus, and Joseph was the father of the others). We know this from Matthew 13:55–56, "Isn't this the carpenter's son? Isn't his mother's name Mary, and aren't his brothers James, Joseph, Simon and Judas? Aren't all his sisters with us?"

- His brother Judas wrote a book in the New Testament, the book of Jude.

- His brother James also wrote one of the books in the New Testament. Guess what it was named. Right . . . James! Judas and James were skeptics until they met with Jesus after his resurrection (John 7:5; Acts 1:14; 1 Cor. 15:7). James became a leader in the Jerusalem church (Acts 12:17; 15:13–21).

2. Beginning of Jesus' _____

Four significant events mark the beginning of Jesus' public ministry at thirty years of age:
- The ministry of John the Baptist (Mark 1:1–8; Luke 3:1–18)
- Jesus' baptism (Matt. 3:13–17; Mark 1:9–11)
- Jesus' temptation in the wilderness (Luke 4:1–13; Matt. 4:1–11)
- Jesus' turning the water to wine (John 2:1–11)

3. Jesus' ministry in _____

Beginning: Cleansing the temple (John 2:13ff)

Ending: Conversation with the woman at the well (John 4:1–42)

Significant Events: Conversation with Nicodemus (John 3)

4. Jesus' ministry in _____

Beginning: Healing the nobleman's son at Capernaum (John 4:46–53)

Ending:
    Peter's statement of trust (Matt. 16:13ff)
    Jesus' Transfiguration (Matt. 17:1ff; Luke 9:28ff)

Significant Events:
    The Sermon on the Mount (Matt. 5–7)
    Calling the disciples (Luke 5:1–11; Mark 2:13–14; Luke 6:12–16)
    Feeding the 5,000 (Matt. 14:13–21; Mark 6:30–44)

5. Jesus' journey to _____

Beginning: He "resolutely set out for" Jerusalem (Luke 9:51)

Ending: Mary anoints his body for burial (John 12:1ff; Matt. 26:6–13)

Significant Events:
    Clashes with the Pharisees (Luke 14; Luke 16:14ff)
    The resurrection of Lazarus (John 11:1ff)
    Meeting Zacchaeus in Jericho (Luke 19:1ff)

6. Jesus' death, burial, and resurrection

Beginning: The triumphal entry into Jerusalem (Matt. 21:1–11)

Ending: The ascension into heaven (Luke 24:50–51)

Significant Events:

Cleansing the temple, the Garden of Gethsemane, trials (Luke 19:45–46; John 17–18)

Jesus dies on the cross (Matt. 27:31–50; Luke 23:26–46)

Jesus is buried in a tomb (Mark 15:42–47; John 19:38–42)

Jesus is alive (Matt. 28:2–15; Mark 16:1–17; Luke 24:1–7; John 20:1–18)

Key Personal Perspective

Jesus is a part of history. In the *Encyclopaedia Britannica,* following a discussion of the writings about Jesus outside of the New Testament, the following statement is made: "These independent accounts prove that in ancient times even the opponents of Christianity never doubted the historicity of Jesus, which was disputed for the first time and on inadequate grounds by several authors at the end of the 18th, during the 19th and at the beginning of the 20th centuries."[2]

> For God so loved the world that he gave his one and only Son, that whoever believes in him shall not perish but have eternal life.
>
> —John 3:16

The eternally existent Christ
What does he look like?

All the evidence points to Jesus still existing in his _____ in heaven:

- He ascended to heaven in bodily form (Acts 1:9).
- He will return in bodily form (Acts 1:11).
- Stephen saw him in bodily form in heaven (Acts 7:55–56).
- Paul indicated Jesus now has a glorious body (Phil. 3:21).

What is he doing?

- He is _____ at God's right hand (Eph. 1:20–22; 1 Peter 3:22).

- He is _____ for us (Rom. 8:34).

- He is holding the _____ together (Col. 1:16–17).

- He is anxiously _____ for us to be with him (John 14:1–3; 17:24).

Acting on the Truth

Jesus Christ wants to be your best friend. Think of it—your best friend is ruling at God's right hand, is the one who holds the universe together. Let me encourage you to enjoy the fact that he is your friend this week by choosing to act as if he is your best friend. Here are three ways you can do that:

1. Say to yourself, "He accepts me even when I don't feel acceptable." Remind yourself throughout this week that you are Jesus' friend because of his grace, not because you somehow deserve that friendship.

2. Talk to him—like a friend. That's what prayer is. At least once this week take a few minutes to tell Jesus what is happening in your life much as you would talk to a best friend. Sure, he already knows what's happening to you. But it is life-changing for you to talk to him as a friend about what you're facing each day.

3. Listen to him—like a friend. When I'm reading the Bible I'm reading the book he gave me. This week, listen as you read. What is God saying to you about his love for you?

Begin working on memory card 3, "The Truth about Jesus."

Discussion Questions

1. What does "having a relationship with Jesus" mean to you?

2. When you get to heaven and come face to face with the eternally existent Jesus:
   - What do you want to say to him?
   - What question do you want to ask him?
   - What emotions do you think you'll experience?

3. Here's the important follow-up: What is it that keeps us from telling him or asking him or feeling those emotions right now? What gets in the way of us sensing that Jesus is our best friend right now? (Talk about ways you may have broken through some of these barriers.)

4. What new thing did you learn about Jesus in this study?

5. At the end of the study we looked at three ways to begin to act on the truth that Jesus is your best friend this next week: remind yourself of his acceptance of you as a friend, talk to him as a friend, or listen to him as a friend. Which of these do you think would best help you to come to a new understanding and appreciation of your friendship with Jesus? Why?

Answers to Fill-Ins

priority	Judea
challenge	Galilee
purpose	Jerusalem
promise	resurrected body
position	ruling
created	praying
ministered	universe
boyhood	waiting
ministry	

Jesus
Part 2

Life Change Objective

To develop an understanding of Jesus' nature as both God and man that will protect you against false teachings and give you confidence in trusting Jesus with a specific need.

What does it mean when we say that Jesus is both man and God?

Is Jesus . . .

- A man who became God?
- God indwelling a man?
- God appearing to be a man?
- A spiritual being ordered by God to become man?
- Fully God and fully man?

    In the beginning was the Word, and the Word was with God, and the Word was God.

    —John 1:1

    Anyone who acknowledges that Jesus Christ came as a human being has the Spirit who comes from God.

    —1 John 4:2 (GNT)

Jesus Is God

How do we know Jesus is God?

1. Jesus said he is God.

    He was even calling God his own Father, making himself equal with God.
    —John 5:18

    I and the Father are one.

    —John 10:30

    Anyone who has seen me has seen the Father.

    —John 14:9

"I tell you the truth," Jesus answered, "before Abraham was born, I am!"
—John 8:58

I am trying here to prevent anyone saying the really foolish thing that people often say about Him: "I am ready to accept Jesus as a great moral teacher, but I don't accept His claim to be God." That is one thing we must not say. A man who was merely a man and said the sort of things Jesus said would not be a great moral teacher. He would either be a lunatic on a level with the man who says he is a poached egg—or else he would be the Devil of Hell. You must make your choice. Either this man was, and is, the Son of God; or else a madman or something worse.... You can try to shut Him up for a fool, you can spit at Him and call Him a demon; or you can fall at His feet and call Him Lord and God. But let us not come up with any patronizing nonsense about His being a great human teacher. He has not left that open to us. He did not intend to.[1]
—C. S. Lewis

Josh McDowell says that Jesus is either "a liar, a lunatic, or the Lord."[2]

2. _____ said he is God.

This started in the prophecies of Jesus' birth before he was born.

And he will be called . . . Mighty God.
—Isaiah 9:6

It continued with those who were closest to him, his own disciples.

So that at the name of Jesus every knee will bow . . . and that every tongue will confess that Jesus Christ is Lord.
—Philippians 2:10–11 (NASB)

Compare Philippians 2:10–11 with what is said of God in Isaiah.

I am God, and there is no other. . . . Before me every knee will bow; by me every tongue will swear.
—Isaiah 45:22–23

For in Christ all the fullness of the Deity lives in bodily form.
—Colossians 2:9

In the beginning was the Word, and the Word was with God, and the Word was God. He was with God in the beginning.
—John 1:1–2

3. He is _____ as God (Matt. 14:33; Phil. 2:10; Heb. 1:6).

- Many worshiped him: a healed leper (Matt. 8:2), women (Matt. 15:25), the mother of James and John (Matt. 20:20), a Gerasenes demoniac (Mark 5:6), a blind man (John 9: 38).

- He accepted such worship (John 20:28–29; Matt. 14:33; 28:9–10).

- His disciples prayed to him (Acts 7:59).

4. He does what _____ can do.

- He has the power to forgive sin (Mark 2:1–12).

- All _____ is in his hands (John 5:27; Acts 17:31).

- He sends the Spirit (John 15:26).

- He will raise the dead (John 5:25).

- He is the _____ (John 1:3; Col. 1:16; Heb. 1:10).

- He is the Sustainer—upholding all (Col. 1:17; Heb. 1:3).

Those are the facts, facts supported by the evidence.

What evidence supports Jesus' claim to be God?

Obviously anyone could "claim" to be God. The difference with Jesus is that his life backs up those claims.

Evidence 1: _____

> [Jesus] said to them, "This is what I told you while I was still with you: Everything must be fulfilled that is written about me in the Law of Moses, the Prophets and the Psalms."
>
> —Luke 24:44

The Old Testament verses are the prophecy. The New Testament verses proclaim the fulfillment.

1. Born of a virgin (Isa. 7:14; Matt. 1:21–23).
2. A descendant of Abraham (Gen. 12:1–3; 22:18; Matt. 1:1; Gal. 3:16).
3. Of the tribe of Judah (Gen. 49:10; Luke 3:23, 33; Heb. 7:14).
4. Of the house of David (2 Sam. 7:12–16; Matt. 1:1).
5. Born in Bethlehem (Mic. 5:2; Matt. 2:1; Luke 2:4–7).
6. Taken to Egypt (Hos. 11:1; Matt. 2:14–15).
7. Herod's killing of the infants (Jer. 31:15; Matt. 2:16–18).
8. Anointed by the Holy Spirit (Isa. 11:2; Matt. 3:16–17).
9. Heralded by the messenger of the Lord (John the Baptist) (Isa. 40:3; Mal. 3:1; Matt. 3:1–3).
10. Would perform miracles (Isa. 35:5–6; Matt. 9:35).
11. Would preach good news (Isa. 61:1; Luke 4:14–21).
12. Would minister in Galilee (Isa. 9:1; Matt. 4:12–16).
13. Would cleanse the temple (Mal. 3:1; Matt. 21:12–13).
14. Would enter Jerusalem as a king on a donkey (Zech. 9:9; Matt. 21:4–9).
15. Would be rejected by Jews (Ps. 118:22; 1 Peter 2:7).

16. Die a humiliating death (Ps. 22; Isa. 53) involving:
    a. rejection (Isa. 53:3; John 1:10–11; 7:5, 48).
    b. betrayal by a friend (Ps. 41:9; Luke 22:3–4; John 13:18).
    c. being sold for thirty pieces of silver (Zech. 11:12; Matt. 26:14–15).
    d. silence before his accusers (Isa. 53:7; Matt. 27:12–14).
    e. being mocked (Ps. 22:7–8; Matt. 27:31).
    f. being beaten (Isa. 52:14; Matt. 27:26).
    g. being spit upon (Isa. 50:6; Matt. 27:30).
    h. piercing his hands and feet (Ps. 22:16; Matt. 27:31).
    i. being crucified with thieves (Isa. 53:12; Matt. 27:38).
    j. praying for his persecutors (Isa. 53:12; Luke 23:34).
    k. piercing his side (Zech. 12:10; John 19:34).
    l. being given gall and vinegar to drink (Ps. 69:21; Matt. 27:34; Luke 23:36).
    m. no broken bones (Ps. 34:20; John 19:32–36).
    n. being buried in a rich man's tomb (Isa. 53:9; Matt. 27:57–60).
    o. casting lots for his garments (Ps. 22:18; John 19:23–24).

17. Would rise from the dead (Ps. 16:10; Mark 16:6; Acts 2:31).

18. Ascend into heaven (Ps. 68:18; Acts 1:9).

19. Would sit down at the right hand of God (Ps. 110:1; Heb. 1:3).

 ## A Closer Look

Some people call this fulfillment of prophecy a "statistical accident." He "just happened" to be born in Bethlehem, to be of David's line, etc. There are two answers to that argument. First, these predictions were more than just a matter of chance. He "just happened" to make a blind man see. He "just happened" to rise again from the dead. That's beyond statistical probability!

The second answer is the large number of prophecies that were fulfilled. Peter Stoner in his book *Science Speaks* has calculated the mathematical probability of even eight of these prophecies being fulfilled in one man.

We find that the chance that any man might have lived down to the present time and fulfilled all eight prophecies is 1 in 10^{17}.

That would be one in 100,000,000,000,000,000. In order for us to be able to comprehend this staggering probability, Stoner illustrates it by supposing that:

> We take 10^{17} silver dollars and lay them on the face of Texas. They will cover all of the state two feet deep. Now mark one of these silver dollars and stir the whole mass thoroughly, all over the state. Blindfold a man and tell him that he can travel as far as he wishes, but he must pick up one silver dollar and say that this is the right one. What chance would he have of getting the right one? Just the same chance that the prophets would have had of writing these eight prophecies and having them all come true in any one man, from their day to the present time, providing they wrote in their own wisdom.[3]

And Jesus did not just fulfill eight prophecies, he fulfilled more than 300 specific prophecies of his life from the Old Testament!

Evidence 2: His _____

When asked for proof, Jesus pointed to the miracles.

> When the men came to Jesus, they said, "John the Baptist sent us to you to ask, 'Are you the one who was to come, or should we expect someone else?'" . . . So he replied to the messengers, "Go back and report to John what you have seen and heard: The blind receive sight, the lame walk, those who have leprosy are cured, the deaf hear, the dead are raised, and the good news is preached to the poor."
>
> —Luke 7:20, 22

"the blind receive sight" (Matt. 9:27–31; Luke 18:35–43; Mark 8:22–26)

"the lame walk" (Matt. 9:2–7)

"those who have leprosy are cured" (Matt. 8:2–3; Luke 17:11–19)

"the deaf hear" (Mark 7:31–37)

"the dead are raised" (Matt. 9:18–19, 23–25; Luke 7:11–15; John 11:1–44)

"good news is preached" (Matt. 11:5)

Evidence 3: His _____

Jesus not only predicted it but told the number of days!

> Jesus answered them, "Destroy this temple, and I will raise it again in three days."
>
> —John 2:19

For as Jonah was three days and three nights in the belly of a huge fish, so the Son of Man will be three days and three nights in the heart of the earth.

—Matthew 12:40

He then began to teach them that the Son of Man must suffer many things and be rejected by the elders, chief priests and teachers of the law, and that he must be killed and after three days rise again.

—Mark 8:31

He claimed the authority behind the Resurrection.

The reason my Father loves me is that I lay down my life—only to take it up again. No one takes it from me, but I lay it down of my own accord. I have authority to lay it down and authority to take it up again. This command I received from my Father.

—John 10:17–18

Jesus Is Man

How do we know that Jesus is man?

1. He had a human _____ (Isa. 7:14–16; Matt. 1:23; Gal. 4:4).

   (A virgin birth)

2. He showed human _____ (Luke 2:52).

   Notice the four human ways that Jesus grew:

   - _____

   - _____

   - _____

   - _____

3. He experienced human _____.

   Jesus felt:
   - Grief (John 11:35)
   - Sorrow (Matt. 26:38)
   - Amazement (Matt. 8:10)
   - Love (for an unbeliever: Mark 10:21; for his friends: John 11:5; for his disciples: John 13:1; for his mother: John 19:26–27)
   - Wonder (Mark 6:6)
   - Distress (Mark 14:33)
   - Compassion (Mark 1:41)
   - Anger (Mark 3:5)

4. He had human _____ and _____.

- He was tired (John 4:6; Mark 4:38).
- He was hungry (Matt. 4:2).
- He was thirsty (John 19:28).
- He was in agony (Luke 22:44).
- He was tempted (Matt. 4:1–11).
- He died (Luke 23:46).

A Fresh Word

Incarnation

The word *incarnation* is from the Latin for "in the flesh." When Jesus was born in Bethlehem, it was the incarnation of God into this world. God came to us in human flesh.

Jesus Is Fully God and Fully Man

The council of Chalcedon was a group called together in 451 A.D. to deal with false teaching in that day as to the nature of Jesus. Look at their famous affirmation of the truth that Jesus is fully God and fully man.

Jesus exists "in two natures which exist without confusion, without change, without division, without separation, the difference of the natures having been in no wise taken away by reason of the union, but rather the properties of each being preserved, and both concurring into one person."

Wow! What does all that mean?

- Jesus became 100 percent God and 100 percent man 100 percent of the time (that's not good math, but it's excellent theology).
- Jesus was not God indwelling a man. He was not a man who became God. He was not God appearing to be a man. He combined in one personality the two natures: he was fully God and he was fully man.
- Jesus is perfect humanity wrapped around undiminished deity.

A Fresh Word

Hypostatic Union

The union of undiminished deity and perfect humanity forever in one person. That means that Jesus not only became God and man but that he will always be God and man.

1. Jesus always has been God (John 1:2).
2. Jesus became man while continuing to be God (John 1:14).
3. Jesus continues to exist as God and man (Acts 1:9–11).

Jesus limited himself—he became fully man.

But . . .

Jesus did not lessen himself—he remained fully God.

Jesus limited himself.

- By taking the form of a man (Phil. 2:6–8)

- By limiting his presence to one place and one time

- By taking a position in which the Father was "greater" (John 14:28)

- By limiting his understanding (Matt. 24:36)

The idea of Jesus being limited and yet also being God is difficult to understand. This is one of those times when it's good to realize that God is so much greater than we are that some of the truths about him are difficult for us to grasp.

Jesus did not lessen himself.

- He was still fully God even as he walked this earth.

- The decision to be born a man, to walk this earth, and to die on a cross was made by him as a part of the Trinity.

Even while on earth, he limited himself by choice: He could have turned the stones to bread when Satan tempted him (Luke 4:3). He could have called 10,000 angels to save him from the cross (Matt. 26:53), but he chose not to.

Key Personal Perspective

Philippians 2:5–11 is one of the most exciting passages in the Bible about Jesus' willingness to become a man. As you read it, note that it says at the beginning, "Your attitude should be the same as that of Christ Jesus." What is Paul talking about? What attitude is revealed in Jesus' willingness to become a man?

Verses 3–4 share several specifics concerning this attitude:

- Do nothing out of selfish ambition.
- Don't act out of vain conceit.
- Consider others better than yourself.
- Don't just look out for yourself.
- Look out for the interests of others.

The attitude is _____.

As fully man, Jesus shows us that he _____ our needs.

As fully God, Jesus shows us that he can _____ our needs.

Finish memorizing memory card 3, "The Truth about Jesus."

Discussion Questions

1. How have your friendships with other believers helped you to see God's love in new and fresh ways?

2. Share your experiences from this last week of acting on the truth that Jesus is our best friend. In what ways did you sense the closeness and friendship of Jesus as a part of your daily life? Where were you frustrated, left wishing you would have remembered how close Jesus is? (Don't be afraid to share your frustrations; it will be an encouragement to others who faced the same feelings this last week.)

3. Which of the three evidences for Jesus being God is the strongest for you? Why do you think this evidence is the most important for you?

4. Even with this evidence, many people still struggle to believe. What's the difference between physical proof and personal faith? Is faith something that we should have without any proof at all? Is proof a guarantee that we will have faith?

5. Which is harder for you to see as real: the fact that Jesus is completely God or the fact that Jesus is completely man?

Generally, unbelievers have a harder time seeing Jesus as being God, and believers have a difficult time seeing the human side of Jesus.

6. We know that Jesus can identify with our struggles and weaknesses because of the fact that he became a person. Right now, what are one or two areas where you are glad he is able to identify with you?

Tiredness   Temptations   Emotions   Disappointment

Betrayal   Relationships   Stress   Other: _____

7. The life of Jesus was all about serving others. Those who get close to him end up being more and more like him, wanting to serve others. Who needs your service in Jesus' name this next week? It doesn't have to be something big or noticeable.

In Matthew 10:42 Jesus says, "And if anyone gives even a cup of cold water to one of these little ones because he is my disciple, I tell you the truth, he will certainly not lose his reward."

This week, look for ways to do seemingly little acts of ministry in Jesus' name. You don't have to *tell* the people you're serving that you're doing it in Jesus' name. "I'm unselfishly bringing you this cup of coffee in the name of my Lord and Savior Jesus Christ!" Not that way! Just do it without calling attention to yourself.

For Further Study

Edersheim, Alfred. *The Life and Times of Jesus the Messiah*. McLean, Va.: MacDonald, n.d.

Elwell, Walter, ed. *Topical Analysis of the Bible*. Grand Rapids, Mich.: Baker, 1991.

Little, Paul. *Know What You Believe*. Wheaton, Ill.: Victor, 1987.

Lucado, Max. *God Came Near*. Portland, Ore.: Multnomah Press, 1987.

McDowell, Josh. *The New Evidence That Demands a Verdict*. Nashville: Nelson Reference, 1999.

Rhodes, Ron. *The Heart of Christianity*. Eugene, Ore.: Harvest House, 1996.

Strobel, Lee. *The Case for Christ*. Grand Rapids, Mich.: Zondervan, 1998.

Yancey, Philip. *The Jesus I Never Knew*. Grand Rapids, Mich.: Zondervan, 1995.

Answers to Fill-Ins

others

worshiped

only God

judgment

Creator

fulfillment of prophecy

miracles

resurrection

birth

growth

intellectually

physically

spiritually

socially

emotions

experiences, needs

humility

understands

meet

The Holy Spirit
Part 1

Life Change Objectives

- To experience a new sense of security in your relationship with God based on the presence of his Spirit in your life.

- To see with eyes of faith how the Holy Spirit is at work in your life.

To most of us, the Holy Spirit seems mysterious. We can't fit him into a human form. The symbols used to represent him in Scripture (oil, fire, wind, dove) don't help much. The Bible teaches us that the Holy Spirit, like God the Father and God the Son, is to be worshiped, loved, and obeyed. We can get to know him personally.

Review of truths about God:

1. God relates to us as a Trinity, three persons in one being.
2. God is one, he is not three gods, but one God (Deut. 6:4).
3. The Father is God, the Son is God, and the Spirit is God.
4. The three are distinct from one another, separate but one.

Historical Background

In the Old Testament the Holy Spirit came upon people at
_____ times for _____ purposes. He
never indwelt anyone _____.

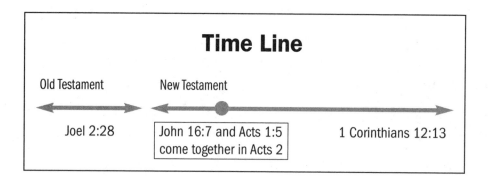

What Is the Role of the Holy Spirit Today?

The Holy Spirit _____ *me.*

Definition: _____

> In reply Jesus declared, "I tell you the truth, no one can see the kingdom of God unless he is born again."
>
> —John 3:3

> He saved us. It was not because of any good deeds that we ourselves had done, but because of his own mercy that he saved us, through the Holy Spirit, who gives us new birth and new life by washing us.
>
> —Titus 3:5 (GNT)

Before I came to Christ, I was _____.

Now I am _____ through the new birth.

> What gives life is God's Spirit; human power is of no use at all. The words I have spoken to you bring God's life-giving Spirit.
>
> —John 6:63 (GNT)

The Holy Spirit _____ *me.*

1. The baptism of the Holy Spirit is the placing of the Christian
   into the _____ and into
   _____.

For we were all baptized by one Spirit into one body—whether Jews or Greeks, slave or free—and we were all given the one Spirit to drink.

—1 Corinthians 12:13

There are 150 New Testament references to our being "in Christ" (Eph. 1:13).

2. The baptism of the Holy Spirit is a _____ occurring at the moment of salvation.

3. The baptism of the Holy Spirit is a _____ _____ for believers.

You are all sons of God through faith in Christ Jesus, for all of you who were baptized into Christ have clothed yourselves with Christ.

—Galatians 3:26–27

For we were all baptized . . . we were all given the one Spirit to drink.

—1 Corinthians 12:13

The baptism of the Holy Spirit is a universal gift to believers. Nowhere in the Bible are Christians instructed to desire or seek the baptism of the Holy Spirit. We should not pray for it, seek it, or try to achieve it. We already have it.

Note: Much of the confusion over the baptism of the Holy Spirit comes about because of the failure to make a distinction between the baptism of the Holy Spirit and the filling of the Holy Spirit. The baptism of the Holy Spirit is something God does for us in establishing our relationship with Jesus Christ. The filling of the Holy Spirit is the daily experience of our yielding to the Holy Spirit's control. We will discuss the filling of the Holy Spirit in detail in the next session.

The Holy Spirit _____ me.

Do you not know that your body is a temple of the Holy Spirit, who is in you, whom you have received from God?

—1 Corinthians 6:19

The Holy Spirit came to live in our lives!

The Holy Spirit _____ me.

And you also were included in Christ when you heard the word of truth, the gospel of your salvation. Having believed, you were marked in him with a seal, the promised Holy Spirit.

—Ephesians 1:13

Sealing implies _____ and _____.

The Holy Spirit is

_____.

...who is a deposit guaranteeing our inheritance until the redemption of those who are God's possession—to the praise of his glory.

—Ephesians 1:14

Now it is God who has made us for this very purpose and has given us the Spirit as a deposit, guaranteeing what is to come.

—2 Corinthians 5:5

If we are faithless, he will remain faithful, for he cannot disown himself.

—2 Timothy 2:13

Key Personal Perspective

1. You may have realized that you have never been born again; you have never experienced the regeneration of the Holy Spirit. Come to God, repent of living life to please yourself, and ask him to give you a new birth and eternal life with him.

2. You may have been confused about the baptism of the Holy Spirit. You've prayed and sought another experience with God that would change you forever. Now you see that the miraculous has already happened to you. Thank God for putting you in Christ where you belong with all in God's family. Thank him that his work is so powerful and complete that you never have to repeat it. Thank God that because you are in Christ, he now sees you covered by Jesus' righteousness. You are pure, spotless, and holy before him.

3. Thank God that his promises are faithful and that his pledge to keep you forever is true. Thank the Holy Spirit for sealing you so that you are safe from losing your salvation. Spend a few moments thinking of the time when you will receive all that has been promised to you; when God's engagement ring becomes a wedding ring, and you will sit with him at the Marriage Supper of the Lamb in heaven.

Begin working on memory card 4, "The Truth about the Holy Spirit."

Appendix

The Holy Spirit began a new work on the Day of Pentecost that has continued up to the present. Before Jesus' resurrection and ascension into heaven, the Holy Spirit came upon people from time to time, but he never actually indwelt or lived inside of a person.

The prophet Joel prophesied that one day God would "pour out [his] Spirit on all people" (Joel 2:28). Jesus promised his disciples that he would send his Spirit to them after he went back to be with the Father.

> But I tell you the truth: It is for your good that I am going away. Unless I go away, the Counselor will not come to you; but if I go, I will send him to you.
>
> —John 16:7

Ten days after Jesus ascended to heaven, 120 believers were gathered in an upper room to wait and pray. Suddenly there came the sound of a rushing wind that filled the place, and separate tongues of fire came to rest on each of the believers. All of them were filled with the Holy Spirit and began to speak in other languages as the Spirit enabled them (Acts 2:1–4).

A little later in the day, as Peter was explaining what had happened to a much larger crowd, he referred to the gift as the "gift of the Holy Spirit." He urged his audience to repent and be baptized and receive the Holy Spirit (Acts 2:38). Peter's understanding of the prophecy of Joel was twofold: not only was salvation promised to those the Lord calls but they also were to receive the gift of the baptism of the Spirit. Three thousand people responded that day and were baptized with water (Acts 2:41).

The three thousand do not seem to have experienced the same miraculous phenomena (rushing wind, tongues of flame, or speaking in other tongues) as the 120 in the Upper Room. What was the difference? The 120 were already believers and received the baptism of the Spirit months or years after they started following Jesus. The three thousand were unbelievers who received the forgiveness of their sins and the gift of the Spirit simultaneously. This distinction is of great importance because the norm for Christian experience today is that of the three thousand, not the 120. The fact that the experience of the 120 was in two distinct stages was simply due to historical circumstances—they could not have received the Pentecostal gift before Pentecost. But on and after the Day of Pentecost, forgiveness of sins and the gift (i.e., baptism) of the Spirit were received together.

Two other "exceptions" that confuse Christians are the accounts found in Acts 8 and Acts 19.

In Acts 8:5–17, Philip preached in Samaria and many believed and were baptized. But what is unusual is that when the apostles at Jerusalem heard about it, they sent Peter and John to verify the experience. One reason is because these believers were Samaritans and at that time Jews had "no dealings with Samaritans" (John 4:9). Their rivalry had lasted for centuries and might have continued, causing great division in the church. Possibly God withheld the gift of his Spirit from the Samaritan believers until two of the leading apostles investigated and, by the laying on of their hands, acknowledged and confirmed the genuineness of the Samaritans' conversion. Neither a two-stage experience nor the laying on of hands is the norm for receiving the Spirit today.

In Acts 19:1–7, the twelve men Paul met do not seem to be Christians. They were called "disciples," but the story reveals they were actually disciples of John the Baptist. Paul asks if they received the Holy Spirit when they believed, indicating that at first he thought they were believers. But they had never heard of the Holy Spirit and that the "One who is to come" was Jesus. Paul not only laid hands on them but first had to baptize them into the name of the Lord Jesus. Can anyone who has never heard of the Holy Spirit, nor been baptized into Christ, nor even apparently believed in him be called a Christian? No. These disciples of John certainly cannot be considered typical of the average Christian today.

We don't get God on an installment plan. God is not three Gods; he is one. You get Jesus when you get God, when you get the Holy Spirit. You don't receive them one at a time. They are three in one; they come together.

The point of the three "comings" of the Holy Spirit in the book of Acts is that God wanted to show that Jews, Samaritans (who had mixed Jewish and Gentile heritage), and Gentiles all had a place in his body. Christianity was not just a Jewish religion. It confirms the truth of Acts 1:8 that the Gospel would go to Jerusalem and Judea, to Samaria, and to the uttermost parts of the earth.

Discussion Questions

1. It's easy to focus in our Christian growth on how far we have to go rather than on how far we have come. Share with others in your group one or two evidences of God's work in your life.

2. Why do you think we fall into thinking of the Holy Spirit as an impersonal (rather than a personal) and even sometimes as a "lesser" part of the Trinity?

3. Look again at John 3:1–16. Why do you think it was so difficult for a religious man like Nicodemus to understand spiritual rebirth? Do Jesus' words to him help you to better grasp what it means to be born of the Spirit?

4. The word *baptized* literally means "totally immersed." What does it mean for you to be totally immersed in the Spirit of God? Does it affect your perspective on other believers when you realize that we're all totally immersed in the Spirit of God?

5. The sealing of the Holy Spirit is a tremendous source of security in our lives as believers. What is one of the areas of your life where you regularly need to draw on that security account?

6. Second Corinthians 3:3 reminds us:

   You show that you are a letter from Christ, . . . written not with ink but with the Spirit of the living God, not on tablets of stone but on tablets of human hearts.
   —2 Corinthians 3:3

   How do you see God "writing on the hearts" of those who are in your group? Take some time to make this a personal expression of encouragement.

   Go around the circle in your group and share with each person, one at a time, "This is one way I see God's Spirit in your life." At least two or three should share with each person. This may feel a little uncomfortable at first, but if we cheer someone for hitting a home run or applaud their getting a promotion at work, how much more important is it to recognize God's work in the lives of others.

Answers to Fill-Ins

various

specific

permanently

regenerates

to give rebirth

spiritually dead

spiritually alive

baptizes

body of Christ

Christ himself

one-time event

universal experience

indwells

seals

ownership, protection

the deposit of God's
   promise

The Holy Spirit
Part 2

Life Change Objectives

- To gain a clear understanding of the difference between the baptism of the Holy Spirit and the filling of the Holy Spirit.

- To immediately begin to recognize and live out the truth that you are filled with God's Spirit.

Review

Before Jesus' resurrection and ascension into heaven, the Holy Spirit would come upon certain individuals at special times for a special reason. He never lived inside of a person permanently. But the Old Testament prophecy of Joel 2:28 was fulfilled on the Day of Pentecost when the Holy Spirit was poured out on believers in Jesus Christ. Since that time, all Christians have been baptized with the Holy Spirit at the moment of salvation.

We looked at four aspects of the Holy Spirit's work in us: regeneration, baptism, indwelling, and sealing.

1. Regeneration means "new birth." When I came to Christ I was given a new birth; I was born again.

2. The baptism of the Holy Spirit is:
    a. God placing me into the body of Christ (the church) and into Christ himself.
    b. A once-for-all-time event which happens at the moment of salvation.
    c. A universal experience for believers (1 Cor. 12:13).
    d. Receiving all of God at one time; I don't receive God one day, Jesus later, and the Holy Spirit at another time. God is a Trinity—three in one.

3. The indwelling of the Spirit means that God comes to personally live in me.

4. To be sealed by the Holy Spirit means that God places his mark of ownership and protection on my life.

5. As a deposit, God's Holy Spirit also guarantees that all that has been promised to me by God will be mine one day.

In this study we'll look together at the filling of the Holy Spirit.

Our Need for the Filling of the Holy Spirit

The Bible says that everyone is in one of three spiritual positions:[1]

The _____ man

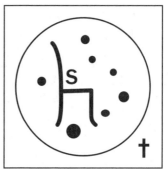

As for you, you were dead in your trans-gressions and sins, in which you used to live when you followed the ways of this world and of the ruler of the kingdom of the air, the spirit who is now at work in those who are disobedient.

—Ephesians 2:1–2

But the man who isn't a Christian can't understand and can't accept these thoughts from God, which the Holy Spirit teaches us. They sound foolish to him, because only those who have the Holy Spirit within them can understand what the Holy Spirit means. Others just can't take it in.

—1 Corinthians 2:14 (LB)

The _____ man

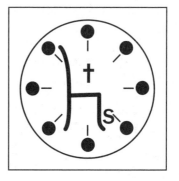

But the spiritual man has insight into everything, and that bothers and baffles the man of the world, who can't under-stand him at all.

—1 Corinthians 2:15 (LB)

The mind of sinful man is death, but the mind controlled by the Spirit is life and peace.

—Romans 8:6

The _____ man

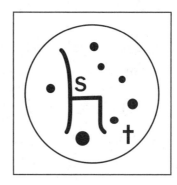

Brothers, I could not address you as spiri-tual but as worldly—mere infants in Christ. I gave you milk, not solid food, for you were not yet ready for it. Indeed, you are still not ready. You are still worldly. For since there is jealousy and quarreling among you, are you not worldly? Are you not acting like mere men?

—1 Corinthians 3:1–3

In Romans 7, the word *I* is used twenty-seven times. In Romans 8 the word *Spirit* is used nineteen times. What made the difference between the defeat that characterizes Paul in Romans 7 and the victory he describes in Romans 8? The filling of the Holy Spirit.

What Is the Filling of the Holy Spirit?

Do not get drunk on wine, which leads to debauchery. Instead, be filled with the Spirit. Speak to one another with psalms, hymns and spiritual songs. Sing and make music in your heart to the Lord, always giving thanks to God the Father for everything, in the name of our Lord Jesus Christ. Submit to one another out of reverence for Christ.

—Ephesians 5:18–21

Four truths from Ephesians 5:18–21

The grammatical construction of these verses implies four truths:

1. The verb used for "filled" is plural, implying
   _____.

2. The verb used for "filled" is present tense (be filled), implying
   _____.

3. The verb used for "filled" is passive, implying the filling is
   _____.

4. The verb for "filled" is imperative, implying
   _____.

Baptism of the Holy Spirit	Filling of the Holy Spirit
A positional* truth	An experiential* truth
Not commanded	Commanded
A one-time event	A continuous event
Puts believer in the position to receive power	Power itself
*Positional truth is who we are because of our faith in Christ. Experiential truth is how we are to live based on that position. One is a root, the other is a fruit.	

Signs of the filling of the Holy Spirit

There is often confusion over "signs" that indicate the Holy Spirit has filled someone. We'll look at this in three sections: experiences that may or may not accompany filling, false ideas about filling, and true signs of the filling of the Spirit.

Personal experiences that may or may not accompany filling

Emotionalism: emotion or feeling is not necessarily part of being filled.

Exceptional ability: God works within the framework of our limitations and natural abilities.

Personal charisma: may be mistaken for filling.

Tranquillity of mind and spirit: great Spirit-filled believers have experienced frustrations, discouragement, and disappointments.

Tongues: throughout history, some Christians speak in tongues when filled, others do not.

False teachings concerning what accompanies filling

Freedom from problems: Filling doesn't make all problems disappear. It does give us the strength and wisdom to better face our problems. The apostle Paul is an example (2 Cor. 6:3–10).

Total freedom from temptation: Jesus faced one of the greatest times of temptation immediately after the Spirit came upon him following his baptism. Some who are filled experience more temptation than when not filled.

Sinless perfection: Obviously this is not true. Every Christian sins and must trust in God's forgiveness and ask for renewed filling every day.

Biblical and universal signs of filling

The gifts of the Spirit:

> A spiritual gift is given to each of us as a means of helping the entire church.
>
> —1 Corinthians 12:7 (NLT)

The fruit of the Spirit:

> But the fruit of the Spirit is love, joy, peace, patience, kindness, goodness, faithfulness, gentleness and self-control.
>
> —Galatians 5:22–23

The power of the Spirit:

> The Holy Spirit gives power to witness (Acts 1:8; Eph. 3:20).

> The apostles were not brash or egotistical, but they had confidence and boldness because of the filling (Acts 4:29).

How Can I Be Filled with the Holy Spirit?

The filling of the Holy Spirit comes when we are cleansed from every known sin and every area of our life is surrendered to Jesus Christ.

> And I will ask the Father, and he will give you another Counselor to be with you forever—the Spirit of truth. The world cannot accept him, because it neither sees him nor knows him. But you know him, for he lives with you and will be in you.
>
> —John 14:16–17

1. _____ for filling and desire it.

> On the last and greatest day of the Feast, Jesus stood and said in a loud voice, "If anyone is thirsty, let him come to me and drink. Whoever believes in me, as the Scripture has said, streams of living water will flow from within him." By this he meant the Spirit, whom those who believed in him were later to receive. Up to that time the Spirit had not been given, since Jesus had not yet been glorified.
>
> —John 7:37–39

2. _____ sins and receive God's cleansing.

> But if we confess our sins to him, he can be depended on to forgive us and to cleanse us from every wrong. (And it is perfectly proper for God to do this for us because Christ died to wash away our sins.)
>
> —1 John 1:9 (LB)

> My people have committed two sins: They have forsaken me, the spring of living water, and have dug their own cisterns, broken cisterns that cannot hold water.
>
> —Jeremiah 2:13

3. _____ to the Holy Spirit's control.

- Let Jesus be Lord daily.

> I have been crucified with Christ and I no longer live, but Christ lives in me. The life I live in the body, I live by faith in the Son of God, who loved me and gave himself for me.
>
> —Galatians 2:20

- Deny self daily.

> Then he called the crowd to him along with his disciples and said: "If anyone would come after me, he must deny himself and take up his cross and follow me. For whoever wants to save his life will lose it, but whoever loses his life for me and for the gospel will save it.
>
> —Mark 8:34–35

4. _____ to fill you as he said he would.

Acting on the Truth

1. Which circle represents your life at this moment? The natural, the spiritual, or the carnal? Probably, like most of us, you would like to "fudge" on this and say, "Well, I know that Christ is in my life, and although he's not Lord in everything, he's Lord in this or that area." The Bible doesn't give us a fourth option: we can't be partially carnal or partially spiritual. At this moment, Jesus is either Lord in all you know and understand of him or he is not. If he is not, will you give the throne in your life back to him?

2. Have you ignored or denied your thirst for God and right relationships? Can you admit your deep thirst today and come to him for the quenching of that thirst? Or have you been trying to dig your own well to satisfy your thirst?

3. What sins have separated you and God from fellowship together? What do you need to confess to him and repent of? Perhaps you need to spend some extended time with God, asking his Holy Spirit to reveal to you where you are wrong so you can trust again in God's forgiveness and ask to be filled again.

4. In what area of your life do you need to trust God for the power to do what he is leading you to do? Where do you need to act in faith? Who do you need to serve? How do you need to use the gifts that God has given you?

> **Finish memorizing memory card 4, "The Truth about the Holy Spirit."**
> **As you put these truths into your heart, expect the Lord to use**
> **them to encourage you, and to encourage others through you.**

Discussion Questions

1. Where do you cross the line between being an imperfect Christian living the Spirit-filled life to being a carnal Christian living a self-centered lifestyle?

2. Some Christian leaders say that up to 95 percent of believers are living worldly lives—lives characterized by some of those struggles we talked about in this session. The question that begs to be asked is why? Discuss in your group two or three reasons why you believe it is so easy and common to settle for less than God's best in our spiritual lives.

3. If you could pick one place in your life where you would like to see God working in greater ways, where would it be?

4. If you could pick one of your character traits that you would like to see God develop in a greater way, what would it be?

5. What does it feel like to be filled with the Holy Spirit? What kinds of thoughts do you have when you're filled with the Spirit?

6. We learned that being filled is something that God does to you. What part, then, do you play in being filled with the Spirit? What is one small thing that you could do *tomorrow* to be more consistently filled with the Spirit?

7. As believers in Christ we cannot live the Christian life on our own power. We must have the daily power and filling of the Holy Spirit. There is likely nothing more important you could do for one another as a group than to be aware of and to pray for one another's needs in this all-important area. Take some time before you leave to make a list of each person's answer to what one thing they could do to more consistently be filled with the Spirit. Copy the list on a 3 x 5 card for each person in your group so you can all pray for each other. The list would look something like this:

> Specific prayer requests for my group—for each one's "one thing" to be more consistently filled with God's Spirit:
>
> John: A daily quiet time
>
> Mary: Trusting in God's forgiveness
>
> Bill: Thinking about God at the beginning of each hour
>
> Ellen: Taking the time to pray for my family
>
> Steve: Choosing to say yes to God
>
> Jan: Seeing the people at my work as people Jesus loves

For Further Study

Bright, Bill. *The Holy Spirit: The Key to Supernatural Living.* San Bernardino, Calif.: Campus Crusade for Christ, 1980.

Elwell, Walter, ed. *Topical Analysis of the Bible.* Grand Rapids, Mich.: Baker, 1991.

Graham, Billy. *The Holy Spirit: Activating God's Power in Your Life.* Dallas: Word, 2000.

Ryrie, Charles Caldwell. *The Holy Spirit.* Chicago: Moody Bible Institute, 1965.

Sanders, J. Oswald. *The Holy Spirit and His Gifts.* Grand Rapids, Mich.: Zondervan, 1973.

Stott, John. *The Baptism and Fullness of the Holy Spirit.* Downers Grove, Ill.: InterVarsity Press, 1964.

Swindoll, Charles R. *Flying Closer to the Flame.* Dallas: Word, 1993.

Answers to Fill-Ins

natural

spiritual

carnal

all are to be filled

repeated action

something done to you

a command

recognize your thirst

repent of your

yield all of yourself

trust God

Creation
Part 1

Life Change Objective

To deepen your conviction that the world and all that is in it are created by the personal action of a personal God.

We study the origins of life because every one of us needs a sense of identity and purpose; what you believe about our origin affects:

_____

_____

_____

In this study we're going to answer three simple questions. Simple to ask, that is. The answers involve who God is, who we are, and why we are here. The three questions are:

1. Why did God create?
2. How did God create?
3. When did God create?

Why Did God Create?

1. God created for _____.

   May the glory of the LORD last forever! The LORD rejoices in all he has made!

   —Psalm 104:31 (NLT)

   All things were created by him and for him.

   —Colossians 1:16

2. God created to express his _____.

> The heavens are yours, and yours also the earth; you founded the world and all that is in it.
>
> —Psalm 89:11

> The earth is the LORD's, and everything in it, the world, and all who live in it.
>
> —Psalm 24:1

3. God created to reflect his _____.

> The heavens declare the glory of God; the skies proclaim the work of his hands. Day after day they pour forth speech; night after night they display knowledge.
>
> —Psalm 19:1–2

> From the time the world was created, people have seen the earth and sky and all that God made. They can clearly see his invisible qualities—his eternal power and divine nature. So they have no excuse whatsoever for not knowing God.
>
> —Romans 1:20 (NLT)

A Closer Look

The Bible is filled with verses that tell us God's creation is an expression of God's character. To look more deeply into this, take some time before the next session to read through these verses.

Neh. 9:5–6; Ps. 19:1–4; Ps. 104:30–32; Isa. 43:7; Rom. 1:20; 2 Cor. 4:6; Ps. 8:1, 3; Ps. 104:24; Isa. 51:12–13, 16; Amos 4:13

---

4. God created to show his _____.

> LORD, you have made many things; with your wisdom you made them all. The earth is full of your riches.
>
> —Psalm 104:24 (NCV)

> By wisdom the LORD laid the earth's foundations, by understanding he set the heavens in place.
>
> —Proverbs 3:19

How Did God Create?

> And God said, "Let there be light," and there was light.
>
> —Genesis 1:3

There are three major views that are important for all believers to understand:

Evolution

This is not a view of "creation" because evolution does not involve a creator. In simplest terms, the view of evolution is that life originated from natural processes, beginning with the first living substance (a single cell) and continuing with the evolving of species.

There is a widespread belief that evolution has been proven by science, thereby making the biblical account of creation untrue.

It is impossible to prove _____ any theory of origins. This is because the scientific method is based on _____ and _____, and it is impossible to make observations or conduct experiments on the origins of the universe.

The problems with the theory of evolution:

1. God is left out of creation.

   Darwin himself rejected the idea of adding intervention by God into the concept of evolution:

   > I will give absolutely nothing for the theory of natural selection if it requires miraculous additions at any one stage of descent.[1]

2. The probability of evolution by _____

   Francis Crick, codiscoverer of the molecular structure of DNA, wrote:

   > This is an easy exercise in combinatorials. Suppose the chain is about two hundred amino acids long; this is, if anything, rather less than the average length of proteins of all types. Since we have just twenty possibilities at each place, the number of possibilities is twenty multiplied by itself some two hundred times. This is conveniently written 20^{200}, that is a one followed by 260 zeros!
   >
   > This number is quite beyond our everyday comprehension. For comparison, consider the number of fundamental particles (atoms, speaking loosely) in the entire visible universe, not just in our own galaxy with its 10^{11} stars, but in all the billions of galaxies, out to the limits of observable space. This number, which is estimated to be 10^{80}, is quite paltry by comparison to 10^{260}. Moreover, we have only considered a polypeptide chain of a rather modest length. Had we considered longer ones as well, the figure would have been even more immense.[2]

   Others write more simply:

   > It requires an incredible amount of faith to believe that evolution could have caused by chance all life that ever did or does now exist.[3]

   > The current scenario of the origin of life is about as likely as the assemblage of a 747 by a tornado whirling through a junkyard.[4]

3. The lack of evidence for species-to-species evolution

Charles Darwin conceded that point, the lack of evidence, in his writings:

> Not one change of species into another is on record. . . . we cannot prove that a single species has been changed.[5]

The Bible tells us that God made each animal "after its kind." This is easily verified not only by the fossil record but also by modern scientific observation and experimentation. Animal breeders have successfully created new breeds of animals but have never changed one species into another.

> We are now about 120 years after Darwin, and knowledge of the fossil record has been greatly expanded. Ironically, we have even fewer examples of evolutionary transition than we had in Darwin's time. By this I mean that some of the classic cases of Darwinian change in the fossil record, such as the evolution of the horse in North America, have had to be discarded or modified as a result of more detailed information.[6]

4. The irreducible _____ of living things

> By irreducibly complex I mean a single system composed of several well-matched, interacting parts that contribute to the basic function, wherein the removal of any one of the parts causes the system to effectively cease functioning. . . . An irreducibly complex biological system, if there is such a thing, would be a powerful challenge to Darwinian evolution.[7]

Theistic evolution

Theistic evolution is the idea that God somehow used the process of evolution as the means by which he created everything.

Although this view is very attractive to all who want to integrate the discoveries of science with the Bible, there are some significant problems with the idea of theistic evolution.

1. The Bible pictures God as being intimately and actively _____ in each aspect and moment of Creation.

> The heavens tell the glory of God, and the skies announce what his hands have made.
>
> —Psalm 19:1 (NCV)

> You alone are the LORD. You made the heavens, even the highest heavens, and all their starry host, the earth and all that is on it, the seas and all that is in them. You give life to everything, and the multitudes of heaven worship you.
>
> —Nehemiah 9:6

By the word of the LORD were the heavens made, their starry host by the breath of his mouth. . . . For he spoke, and it came to be; he commanded, and it stood firm.

—Psalm 33:6, 9

The problem with any form of theistic evolution . . . is that it means design by chance. That's like a square circle. There is no such thing. Blending evolution with creation is like putting a square peg in a round hole. It just doesn't fit.[8]

2. A _____ rather than _____ view of Genesis 1–11

We must realize that the book of Genesis is the foundation of the entire Bible. The word Genesis means "beginnings." Genesis tells the story of the beginning of the universe, solar system, earth, life, man, sin, Israel, nations, and salvation. An understanding of Genesis is crucial to our understanding of the rest of Scripture.

For example, Genesis chapters 1–11 are quoted or referred to more than 100 times in the New Testament alone. And it is over these chapters that the primary battle for the historicity of Genesis rages. All of the first eleven chapters are referred to in the New Testament. Every New Testament author refers somewhere to Genesis 1–11. . . .

How can the first 11 chapters be separated from even the rest of Genesis? The time of Abraham has been verified by archeology. The places, customs, and religions spoken of in Genesis related to Abraham are accurate. The story of Abraham begins in Genesis 12. If Genesis 1 is mythology and Genesis 12 history, where does the allegory stop and the history begin in the first 11 chapters? It is all written in the same historical narrative style.[9]

3. Placing God's _____ and God's _____ on equal footing as revelations of God

While the heavens do "tell the glory of God," they cannot do so as faithfully and clearly as the Bible.

The grass withers and the flowers fall, but the word of our God stands forever.

—Isaiah 40:8

Heaven and earth will pass away, but my words will never pass away.
—Matthew 24:35

Supernatural Creation

God personally and supernaturally created the heavens and the earth.

Science may provide reasonable evidence, but ultimately it is a matter of faith.

1. Science shows us the big bang, but it takes faith to believe God said, "Let there be light."

   Science can point to a creator.

   • On May 4, 1992, *Time* magazine reported that NASA's Cosmic Background Explorer satellite—COBE—had discovered landmark evidence that the universe did in fact begin with the primeval explosion that has become known as the Big Bang. "If you're religious, it's like looking at God," proclaimed the leader of the research team, George Smoot.[10]

   But only by faith can we believe in our Creator.

   • In Genesis 1:3 the Bible says, "And God said, 'Let there be light,' and there was light."

2. Science shows us the intelligent design of the universe, but it takes faith to believe God personally created that universe.

   Science can point to a creator.

   • A July 20, 1998, *Newsweek* article entitled "Science Finds God" reported:

     Physicists have stumbled on signs that the cosmos is custom-made for life and consciousness. It turns out that if the constants of nature—unchanging numbers like the strength of gravity, the charge of an electron and the mass of a proton—were the tiniest bit different, then atoms would not hold together, stars would not burn and life would never have made an appearance. "When you realize that the laws of nature must be incredibly finely tuned to produce the universe we see," says John Polkinghorne, who had a distinguished career as a physicist at Cambridge University before becoming an Anglican priest in 1982, "that conspires to plant the idea that the universe did not just happen, but that there must be a purpose behind it." Charles Townes, who shared the 1964 Nobel Prize in Physics for discovering the principles of the laser, goes further: "Many have a feeling that somehow intelligence must have been involved in the laws of the universe."[11]

   But only by faith can we believe in our Creator.

   • In Genesis 1:1 the Bible says, "In the beginning God created the heavens and the earth."

     A sound explanation may exist for the explosive birth of our Universe; but if it does, science cannot find out what the explanation is. The scientist's pursuit of the past ends in the moment of creation. This is an exceedingly strange development, unexpected by all but the theologians. They have always accepted the word of the Bible: In the beginning God created heaven and earth. . . . For the scientist who has lived by his faith in the power of reason, the story ends like a bad dream. He has scaled the mountains of ignorance; he is about to conquer the highest peak; as he pulls himself over the final rock, he is greeted by a band of theologians who have been sitting there for centuries.[12]

—Robert Jastrow, founder of NASA's Goddard
Institute for Space Studies

When Did God Create?

1. All evolutionists believe that Earth is _____.

2. Creationists are divided; most believe in a _____, but there are some who believe it is an _____.

The debate between these views centers around the translation of the word *day* (*yom* in Hebrew) in the Genesis 1 text. *Yom* can mean any of the following:

1. A 24-hour day, which is the most common usage in the Old Testament

2. An unspecified period of time

3. An era

A Closer Look

Two Questions

1. How could "old earth" creationists believe that the earth is billions of years old when the Bible says that God created it in just six days?

   They believe that the days detailed in Genesis 1 represent millions of years or that there was a significant gap between the days of Creation.

2. How could "young earth" creationists believe that the earth is thousands of years old in light of the scientific evidence?

   They believe that God created the universe in full working order —with the starlight already reaching the earth and the ecosystem fully mature. They believe that this fact (along with the cataclysm caused by a worldwide flood) calls into question the apparent time lines deduced from radioactive dating, the earth's magnetic field, petroleum gas deposits, planet rotations, etc.

The major theological question concerning when God created is, When did sin and death enter the world?

Since...

> The Bible tells us that it was Adam's personal choice to sin that brought death and the fall of creation.

> When Adam sinned, sin entered the entire human race. Adam's sin brought death, so death spread to everyone, for everyone sinned.
>
> —Romans 5:12 (NLT)

> Romans 8:20 tells us that the whole of creation suffers because of Adam's sin. Our sin infected all of creation.

And since...

> The salvation that Jesus brings to us is tied in the New Testament to the historical fact of Adam's sin.

> For since death came through a man, the resurrection of the dead comes also through a man. For as in Adam all die, so in Christ all will be made alive.
>
> —1 Corinthians 15:21–22

Therefore...

> Any idea of creation that theorizes the death of human beings and the fall of God's creation before the sin of Adam and Eve is contrary to the clear teaching of God's Word.

Acting on the Truth

1. Today will you settle the matter of who made you and the world? Will you believe what God says about himself? And then will you determine to let his Word set the agenda for your life?

2. Today will you refresh your belief (or believe for the first time) that God's creation of you means that you have significance and importance to him?

3. Today will you make a fresh commitment to stand for the truth that God is the personal Creator of all that we see?

4. Every day this week, praise and worship God for all his mighty works. As you drive or walk, enjoy the beauty you see. As you work, enjoy the abilities that God has given you. As you spend time with others, enjoy the unique and marvelous ways that God has made each of us.

Begin working on memory card 5, "The Truth about Creation."

Discussion Questions

1. One of the statements at the beginning of our study of Creation was, "What you believe about your origin affects your self-worth, your relationships, and how you view God." In what ways do you feel that your view of God as our Creator is impacting your daily thoughts about yourself and this world?

2. What is it that amazes you—simply amazes you—about the creation of God?

3. How can we discuss Creation in such a way that we don't appear scientifically illiterate? What are some ways that we can express to others that we are not ignoring the seeming evidence but just seeing it differently?

4. Does a discussion of topics such as irreducible complexity and fossil records excite you or bore you to tears? Why do you think people are different on this point: why do some love to study these details while others could happily do without them?

5. What one thing could you do to advance the idea of God as Creator and God's Word as reliable above the idea of evolution? In your community? With other believers? In your own family?

 Answers to Fill-Ins

your self-worth	chance
your relationships	complexity
how you view God	involved
his own sake	poetic
sovereignty	historical
character	creation
wisdom	Word
scientifically	billions of years old
observation	young earth
experimentation	old planet

Creation
Part 2

Life Change Objective

To build a strong foundation for worshiping and obeying God as your Creator.

Seven Truths about Creation That Are Foundations for Our Lives

God Created Everything out of _____

> By faith we understand that the universe was formed at God's command, so that what is seen was not made out of what was visible.
>
> —Hebrews 11:3

> And God said, "Let there be light," and there was light.
>
> —Genesis 1:3

God simply spoke, and Creation happened.

This week, let the truth about Creation fill you with the wonder you need to face the realities of life.

Creation Was Done in _____

> God said, "Let there be light" . . . God called the expanse "sky" . . . "Let the water under the sky be gathered to one place, and let dry ground appear. . . . Let the land produce vegetation." . . . The land produced vegetation: plants bearing seed according to their kinds and trees bearing fruit with seed in it according to their kinds. . . . "Let there be lights in the expanse of the sky to separate the day from the night, and let them serve as signs to mark seasons and days and years. . . . Let the water teem with living creatures, and let birds fly above the earth. . . . Let the land produce living creatures according to their kinds. . . . Let us make man in our image."
>
> —Genesis 1:3–26

- Both evolutionists and creationists believe in a well-ordered creation.

- Evolution is the idea that order evolved out of chaos.

- The Bible teaches instead that order was created by design.

This week: Let God's creation be a constant reminder that God has a plan!

God Saw That It Was _____

God saw that the light was good, and he separated the light from the darkness.

—Genesis 1:4

God called the dry ground "land," and the gathered waters he called "seas." And God saw that it was good.

—Genesis 1:10

The land produced vegetation: plants bearing seed according to their kinds and trees bearing fruit with seed in it according to their kinds. And God saw that it was good.

—Genesis 1:12

. . . to govern the day and the night, and to separate light from darkness. And God saw that it was good.

—Genesis 1:18

So God created the great creatures of the sea and every living and moving thing with which the water teems, according to their kinds, and every winged bird according to its kind. And God saw that it was good.

—Genesis 1:21

God made the wild animals according to their kinds, the livestock according to their kinds, and all the creatures that move along the ground according to their kinds. And God saw that it was good.

—Genesis 1:25

God saw all that he had made, and it was very good. And there was evening, and there was morning—the sixth day.

—Genesis 1:31

- God's creation is not evil. The world did not make people evil; people brought evil into the world.

- Don't make the mistake of thinking that because something is of the physical world it must therefore be evil.

God richly gives us everything to enjoy.

—1 Timothy 6:17 (NCV)

This week: enjoy God's creation!

Man Is the _____

How exactly did God create man?

> Then the LORD God took dust from the ground and formed a man from it. He breathed the breath of life into the man's nose, and the man became a living person.
>
> —Genesis 2:7 (NCV)

> So the LORD God caused the man to sleep very deeply, and while he was asleep, God removed one of the man's ribs. Then God closed up the man's skin at the place where he took the rib. The LORD God used the rib from the man to make a woman, and then he brought the woman to the man.
>
> —Genesis 2:21–22 (NCV)

How are we created in God's image?

1. Our _____: mind, will, emotions

2. Our _____: created as male and female

> So God created man in his own image, in the image of God he created him; male and female he created them.
>
> —Genesis 1:27

A Closer Look

Because *all* mankind was made in the image of God:

Both _____ and _____ have equal value and worth.

Each _____ has equal value and worth.

> From one man he made every nation of men, that they should inhabit the whole earth; and he determined the times set for them and the exact places where they should live. God did this so that men would seek him and perhaps reach out for him and find him, though he is not far from each one of us. "For in him we live and move and have our being."
>
> —Acts 17:26–28

---

3. Our _____: created as moral beings, with a moral consciousness

> Then the eyes of both of them were opened, and they realized they were naked; so they sewed fig leaves together and made coverings for themselves.
>
> —Genesis 3:7

> So I strive always to keep my conscience clear before God and man.
>
> —Acts 24:16

Our moral nature includes both freedom of choice and responsibility for our choices.

4. Our _____: created with the ability to relate to God

> Now we rejoice in our wonderful new relationship with God—all because of what our Lord Jesus Christ has done in dying for our sins—making us friends of God.
>
> —Romans 5:11 (LB)

This week: intentionally focus throughout each day on the fact that you are made in God's image.

God _____ the Job

> Thus the heavens and the earth were completed in all their vast array.
>
> —Genesis 2:1

> God's work was finished from the time he made the world.
>
> —Hebrews 4:3 (NCV)

- The universe is not some vast unfinished symphony.

- This world and universe are not works in progress.

- The universe is a finished work of creation that has been marred by the presence of sin.

This week: look forward to God's restoration of his creation.

God _____ on the Seventh Day

> By the seventh day God had finished the work he had been doing; so on the seventh day he rested from all his work. And God blessed the seventh day and made it holy, because on it he rested from all the work of creating that he had done.
>
> —Genesis 2:2–3

Why did God rest?

- To give us an _____ to follow

> Work and get everything done during six days each week, but the seventh day is a day of rest to honor the LORD your God. . . . The reason is that in six days the LORD made everything—the sky, the earth, the sea, and everything in them. On the seventh day he rested.
>
> —Exodus 20:9–11 (NCV)

- To teach us his plan for the ages

> There remains, then, a Sabbath-rest for the people of God; for anyone who enters God's rest also rests from his own work, just as God did from his. Let us, therefore, make every effort to enter that rest.
>
> —Hebrews 4:9–11

This week: take a day of worshipful rest.

God Now Sustains All That He Made

> He existed before everything else began, and he holds all creation together.
>
> —Colossians 1:17 (NLT)

The word used for God's continuing and active work in holding creation together is the "providence" of God. Never make the mistake of thinking that God made it all and then somehow left it to run on its own. There are literally hundreds of verses throughout the Bible concerning God's intimate and intricate sustaining of his creation.

From the smallest dewdrop to the greatest nations, God sustains it all!

> Who fathers the drops of dew?
>
> —Job 38:28

> God reigns over the nations; God is seated on his holy throne.
>
> —Psalm 47:8

This week, look to the God who sustains the universe to give you sustaining strength throughout each day.

Acting on the Truth

How to Praise God as Your Creator

"Seeing creation as an expression of your love . . ."

> He made the sun and the moon. His love continues forever. He made the sun to rule the day. His love continues forever. He made the moon and stars to rule the night. His love continues forever. . . . He gives food to every living creature. His love continues forever.
>
> —Psalm 136:7–9, 25 (NCV)

"I kneel before you in humility . . ."

> Come, kneel before the Lord our Maker, for he is our God. We are his sheep, and he is our Shepherd. Oh, that you would hear him calling you today and come to him!
>
> —Psalm 95:6–7 (LB)

"praising you for this day . . ."

> This is the day the LORD has made; let us rejoice and be glad in it.
>
> —Psalm 118:24

"and thanking you for creating me."

> I praise you because you made me in an amazing and wonderful way. What you have done is wonderful. I know this very well.
>
> —Psalm 139:14 (NCV)

> **Finish memorizing memory card 5, "The Truth about Creation"—you'll be amazed at how often you'll share this particular truth!**

Discussion Questions

1. What stands out in your mind as one of the most powerful pictures of the creative mind of God? Be specific.

2. In what ways does God's creation speak to you specifically about the person and character of God? Example: when I look at the stars . . . at the ocean . . . at the Grand Canyon, etc.

3. How does the truth that God is the Creator help you to look at this world with a greater sense of security?

4. Do you tend to look at material things as "good" or as "evil"? Discuss the difference between recognizing that evil is present in this world and thinking that *everything* that is material must be evil.

5. What feelings do you have when you focus your thoughts on the truth that mankind is created in God's image?

6. How well are you doing at following God's example to rest? What are one or two practical things that you could do to better follow his example? (We know, this question *assumes* we aren't doing so well!)

For Further Study

Geisler, Norman L. *Origin Science*. Grand Rapids, Mich.: Baker, 1987.

Ham, Ken. *The Genesis Solution*. Grand Rapids, Mich.: Baker, 1988.

Ham, Ken. *The Lie: Evolution*. El Cajon, Calif.: Creation Life, 1987.

Huse, Scott M. *The Collapse of Evolution*. Grand Rapids, Mich.: Baker, 1983.

McGowan, C. H. *In Six Days*. Van Nuys, Calif.: Bible Voice, 1976.

Morris, Henry. *The Beginning of the World*. El Cajon, Calif.: Creation Life, 1991.

Ross, Hugh. *Creation and Time*. Colorado Springs: NavPress, 1994.

Ross, Hugh. *The Fingerprint of God*. Orange, Calif.: Promise, 1989.

Stoner, Don. *A New Look at an Old Earth*. Eugene, Ore.: Harvest House, 1997.

Answers to Fill-Ins

nothing

proper order

good

crown of creation

personality

sexuality

male, female

race

morality

spirituality

finished

rested

example

Salvation

Part 1

Life Change Objectives

To give you an understanding of God's gift of salvation that enables you to:

- Love God more deeply for what he did for you.

- Tell others more confidently what God can do for them.

The major theme of the Bible is God's eternal plan to rescue us from our sin through Jesus' birth, his death on the cross, and his resurrection.

God knew from the beginning that his creation would need a Savior, so he set in motion all that would be necessary to accomplish the salvation of his children.

While the message of the cross is a familiar one to many, we must guard against attitudes of complacency, boredom, forgetfulness, and, most of all, "I've heard it before." There are so many layers of truth about Christ's work on the cross that we can never come to the point where there is nothing more to learn.

In the study today we will be concentrating on:

The problem: the need for salvation

The provision: the solution of salvation

In the next session we will look at:

The promise: the security of salvation

The Problem: Man's Need for Salvation

To understand man's need for salvation we must look at two things: the nature of God and the nature of man.

The nature of God

We underestimate our need for a Savior because we underestimate who God is.

1. God is _____.

   For this is what the high and lofty One says—he who lives forever, whose name is holy: "I live in a high and holy place, but also with him who is contrite and lowly in spirit, to revive the spirit of the lowly and to revive the heart of the contrite."

   —Isaiah 57:15

   Exalt the LORD our God and worship at his holy mountain, for the LORD our God is holy.

   —Psalm 99:9

   Your eyes are too pure to look on evil; you cannot tolerate wrong.
   —Habakkuk 1:13

   God cannot tolerate anything that is evil.

2. God is _____.

   Holiness has more to do with God's character.

   Righteousness and justice have to do with God's dealings with mankind in relation to his character.

   The LORD is gracious and righteous; our God is full of compassion.
   —Psalm 116:5

   The Lord is fair in everything he does, and full of kindness.
   —Psalm 145:17 (LB)

The nature of man

1. Our nature: we are sinful.

   The Bible records Adam and Eve's sinful choice to disobey God's instructions not to eat from the tree of the knowledge of good and evil (Gen. 2:17; 3). Without knowing it, they unleashed the onslaught of evil and decay that permeates our world today. God cursed them and all of their offspring.

2. Our choice: we sin.

   God says that all of us are considered guilty because of our relationship to Adam and because of our own choices (Rom. 5:18–19; 3:10–18).

3. Our condition: we are lost (Luke 19:10).

A Closer Look

What Are the Consequences of Sin and Lostness?

- Sentenced to physical and spiritual death (Gen. 3:19; John 3:18; Rom. 6:23)

- Separated from God (Eph. 2:12)

- Dominated and controlled by sin (Eph. 2:1–3; Rom. 6:6)

- Spiritual blindness (2 Cor. 4:3–4)

- Without understanding (Rom. 3:11)

- Enemies of Christ (Matt. 12:30)

- Objects of God's wrath (Eph. 2:3)

- Considered children of the Devil (John 8:44)

The Bible portrays mankind's lostness as the most pitiful condition imaginable. Not only is our life on earth wasted as we live for self and selfish desires but the consequence is eternal separation from God (Rom. 6:23; Luke 13:3; Matt. 25:46).

The Provision: God's Solution to Sin

God's solution is the last three words in this verse: faith in Jesus.

> God presented him as a sacrifice of atonement, through faith in his blood. He did this to demonstrate his justice, because in his forbearance he had left the sins committed beforehand unpunished—he did it to demonstrate his justice at the present time, so as to be just and the one who justifies those who have faith in Jesus.
>
> —Romans 3:25–26

Three central truths about how we are saved

1. Salvation is not by works but by _____.

> For it is by grace you have been saved, through faith—and this not from yourselves, it is the gift of God—not by works, so that no one can boast.
>
> —Ephesians 2:8–9

2. Salvation is not initiated by us, but by _____.

It's not man reaching _____ to God, but God reaching _____ to man.

When we were unable to help ourselves, at the moment of our need, Christ died for us, although we were living against God. Very few people will die to save the life of someone else. Although perhaps for a good person someone might possibly die. But God shows his great love for us in this way: Christ died for us while we were still sinners.

—Romans 5:6–8 (NCV)

3. Salvation is not an afterthought with God; it is his _____ _____.

You were bought . . . with the precious blood of Christ, who was like a pure and perfect lamb. Christ was chosen before the world was made, but he was shown to the world in these last times for your sake.

—1 Peter 1:18–20 (NCV)

It is God who saved us and chose us to live a holy life. He did this not because we deserved it, but because that was his plan long before the world began—to show his love and kindness to us through Christ Jesus.

—2 Timothy 1:9 (NLT)

Seven descriptions of salvation

1. _____: Jesus died in my place.

For Christ died for sins once for all, the righteous for the unrighteous, to bring you to God. He was put to death in the body but made alive by the Spirit.

—1 Peter 3:18

- He was made sin for me (2 Cor. 5:21).

- He bore my sin in his body on the cross (1 Peter 2:24).

- He suffered once to bear the sins of others (Heb. 9:28).

- He was tortured for others' sin (Isa. 53:4–6).

- He was made a curse for me (Gal. 3:13).

I have been crucified with Christ and I no longer live, but Christ lives in me. The life I live in the body, I live by faith in the Son of God, who loved me and gave himself for me.

—Galatians 2:20

2. _____: Jesus made me right with God.

Through him everyone who believes is justified from everything you could not be justified from by the law of Moses.

—Acts 13:39

He was delivered over to death for our sins and was raised to life for our justification.

—Romans 4:25

3. _____: Jesus made peace with God possible.

> God was in Christ, making peace between the world and himself. . . . God did not hold the world guilty of its sins. And he gave us this message of peace.
>
> —2 Corinthians 5:19 (NCV)

> For if, when we were God's enemies, we were reconciled to him through the death of his Son, how much more, having been reconciled, shall we be saved through his life!
>
> —Romans 5:10

Jesus is the bridge between God and man.

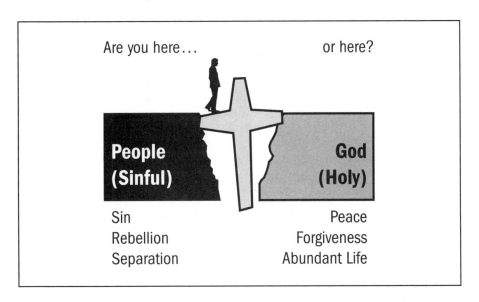

4. _____: Jesus made me a part of God's family.

> He predestined us to be adopted as his sons through Jesus Christ, in accordance with his pleasure and will.
>
> —Ephesians 1:5

> And since we are his children, we will share his treasures—for all God gives to his Son Jesus is now ours too.
>
> —Romans 8:17 (LB)

> For you did not receive a spirit that makes you a slave again to fear, but you received the Spirit of sonship. And by him we cry, "*Abba*, Father."
>
> —Romans 8:15

5. _____: Jesus purchased my salvation with his blood.

A Fresh Word

Redemption

The Greek word for redemption refers to slaves being purchased in the marketplace. In the spiritual sense, all of us were slaves to sin until Jesus purchased us out of the slave market and set us free from sin's bondage. Because he bought and paid for us with his blood, we now belong exclusively to him.

For he has rescued us from the dominion of darkness and brought us into the kingdom of the Son he loves, in whom we have redemption, the forgiveness of sins.

—Colossians 1:13–14

God paid a ransom to save you from the impossible road to heaven which your fathers tried to take, and the ransom he paid was not mere gold or silver, as you very well know. But he paid for you with the precious lifeblood of Christ, the sinless, spotless Lamb of God.

—1 Peter 1:18–19 (LB)

6. _____: Jesus satisfied God's justice.

A Fresh Word

Propitiation

To propitiate is to bring satisfaction or to fulfill a demand or requirement. In heathen circles it was a word that meant "to appease the gods." The biblical sense of the word speaks of that which satisfies the justice of God so that mercy is given.

The picture of propitiation in the Old Testament is the "mercy seat," the cover of the ark of the covenant in first the tabernacle and later the temple. This is the place where blood was sprinkled as an offering for the sins of the people.

He is the atoning sacrifice for our sins, and not only for ours but also for the sins of the whole world.

—1 John 2:2

This is love: not that we loved God, but that he loved us and sent his Son as an atoning sacrifice for our sins.

—1 John 4:10

7. _____: Jesus sent my sins away from me.

> In him we have redemption through his blood, the forgiveness of sins, in accordance with the riches of God's grace.
>
> —Ephesians 1:7

> When you were dead in your sins and in the uncircumcision of your sinful nature, God made you alive with Christ. He forgave us all our sins.
>
> —Colossians 2:13

> As far as the east is from the west, so far has he removed our transgressions from us.
>
> —Psalm 103:12

> You will throw away all our sins into the deepest part of the sea.
>
> —Micah 7:19 (NCV)

Three aspects of salvation: past, present, and future

1. In the _____, I was saved from the _____ of sin (justification).

2. In the _____, I am being saved from the _____ of sin (sanctification).

3. In the _____, I will be saved from the _____ of sin (glorification).

This means that while Jesus' death accomplished all that God intended it to—Jesus said, "It is finished"—we have not experienced all there is to experience of salvation. There is more to look forward to!

Key Personal Perspective

Does someone have to be able to understand all the truths we've discussed today to be saved? No.

To be saved you need to know only three truths:

1. I am a sinner.
2. Jesus died in my place.
3. If I ask God to forgive me for rebelling against him and I trust in Jesus as my Lord, he will save me.

No one can say these three truths are difficult to understand. The truth of our salvation is simple enough for a child to understand, yet deep enough to study the rest of your life and never fully comprehend.

The bottom line question: Have you accepted God's gift of forgiveness for your sin, paid for by Jesus' death on the cross?

Begin working on memory card 6, "The Truth about Salvation."

Appendix

Supplemental Resource

The doctrine of election and predestination is one of the most difficult doctrines that Christians try to understand. In simple terms, election means to choose certain people for a certain purpose, just as we elect government officials. Spiritual election addresses the question of how God chooses us for salvation.

There are two main streams of thought concerning election: Calvinism and Arminianism. Calvinism (named after John Calvin, a sixteenth-century theologian), emphasizes words like *elect, chosen,* or *predestine.* Calvinists typically believe that only certain people are chosen to be saved, and that God passes over the non-elect. They base their views on verses like 1 Peter 1:1–2.

> Peter, an apostle of Jesus Christ, To God's elect, strangers in the world, scattered throughout Pontus, Galatia, Cappadocia, Asia and Bithynia, who have been chosen according to the foreknowledge of God the Father, through the sanctifying work of the Spirit, for obedience to Jesus Christ and sprinkling by his blood: Grace and peace be yours in abundance.
>
> —1 Peter 1:1–2

Arminianism (named after James Arminius, another sixteenth-century theologian) emphasizes words like "whosoever" and "not willing that any should perish." It bases its views on verses like John 3:16 and 2 Peter 3:9. Arminians typically believe in free will and that God in his foreknowledge sees who will respond with faith in Christ and then elects them based on that foreknowledge.

> The Lord is not slow in keeping his promise, as some understand slowness. He is patient with you, not wanting anyone to perish, but everyone to come to repentance.
>
> —2 Peter 3:9

We believe that Scripture teaches both truths, and to exclude one set of verses or emphasize one over the other is unbalanced. God allows us the freedom to choose to love him or not. Our freedom to choose cannot supercede the sovereign election of God. These are ideas that are difficult to reconcile with our finite minds. In the end it must be a matter of trust.

The most frightening thought that haunts some is this: "What if I want God but he doesn't want me?" The truth is, that will never happen! If there is a desire for God in your heart, you're one of the elect!

Discussion Questions

1. What simply amazes you about God's salvation?

2. Do you think any of us felt as lost as we truly were before we were saved? Have you seen any examples that show that the more lost someone knows they were the more appreciative they are of the gift of salvation?

3. The truth of justification is difficult for many to understand. What causes us to struggle to see ourselves as not guilty before God? What is it that has helped you to increase your faith in God's promise that we are justified?

4. In what ways do we take credit for or become prideful concerning the gift of salvation? What has encouraged you to keep before you daily the truth that salvation is completely by grace?

5. The seven pictures of salvation that we looked at in this study are among the greatest treasures in any of our lives.

    1. Substitution: Jesus died in my place.
    2. Justification: Jesus made me right with God.
    3. Reconciliation: Jesus made peace with God possible.
    4. Adoption: Jesus made me a part of God's family.
    5. Redemption: Jesus purchased my salvation with his blood.
    6. Propitiation: Jesus satisfied God's justice.
    7. Forgiveness: Jesus sent my sins away from me.

    Which of these has the most immediate emotional impact on you?

    Which of these would you like to understand better?

    Which could you use to help someone you know to better understand how to become a believer?

Answers to Fill-Ins

holy

righteous and just

grace

God

up

down

eternal plan

substitution

justification

reconciliation

adoption

redemption

propitiation

forgiveness

past

penalty

present

power

future

presence

Salvation
Part 2

Life Change Objective

To give you an assurance of your salvation that results in a deepening security in God's love and an appreciation for God's grace.

Review

- The major theme of the Bible is God's eternal plan to rescue us from the penalty, power, and presence of sin through the death and resurrection of his Son, Jesus.

- God's nature is holy, righteous, and just. Man is sinful both by nature and by choice. God's solution? He has provided us a Savior!

- We looked at seven descriptions of what Jesus did for us on the cross:

  1. Substitution: Jesus died in my place.
  2. Justification: Jesus made me right with God.
  3. Reconciliation: Jesus made peace with God possible.
  4. Adoption: Jesus made me a part of God's family.
  5. Redemption: Jesus purchased my salvation with his blood.
  6. Propitiation: Jesus fully satisfied God's justice.
  7. Forgiveness: Jesus sent my sins away from me.

Even though God has provided us with all of these riches, many Christians remain unsure of their salvation. Last time we looked at the problem (our need for salvation) and the provision (the solution of salvation). In this session we'll look at how to be confident of your salvation.

Why Do So Many People Lack the Assurance of Salvation?

- Because they cannot pinpoint a _____ when they received Christ.[1]

- Because they question the _____ of the way they expressed faith in Christ.

  "Did I pray the right prayer? Did I know everything I needed to know? Should I have felt differently?"

- Because of _____ they commit after salvation.

  There is a difference between the personal assurance of my salvation and the promised security of my salvation. While I may or may not have a *feeling* of assurance, security is a *fact* based on the promise of God. In this study, we're going to look at how God's promise of salvation can deepen our confidence in our salvation.

The Promised Security of Salvation

Each member of the Trinity plays a part in our security as believers.

The sovereign decision of the _____

- God has declared us "not guilty" in his sight and canceled the punishment that should have been ours.

  I tell you the truth, whoever hears my word and believes him who sent me has eternal life and will not be condemned; he has crossed over from death to life.

  —John 5:24

  For God so loved the world that he gave his one and only Son, that whoever believes in him shall not perish but have eternal life. . . . Whoever believes in him is not condemned, but whoever does not believe stands condemned already because he has not believed in the name of God's one and only Son.

  —John 3:16, 18

- God is at peace with me; the war between us is over.

  Therefore, since we have been made right in God's sight by faith, we have peace with God because of what Jesus Christ our Lord has done for us.

  —Romans 5:1 (NLT)

- God has determined that nothing can ever separate me from his love.

For I am convinced that neither death nor life, neither angels nor demons, neither the present nor the future, nor any powers, neither height nor depth, nor anything else in all creation, will be able to separate us from the love of God that is in Christ Jesus our Lord.

—Romans 8:38–39

The high-priestly work of _____

A Closer Look

In the Old Testament sacrificial system, the high priest was the highest spiritual leader. He alone got to enter the Holy of Holies and put blood on the mercy seat once a year on the Day of Atonement. Jesus is our High Priest. When Jesus died on the cross, he was both the ultimate sacrifice and the ultimate sacrificer. He lives forever to do the work of a high priest—to be our intercessor and our mediator.

- Jesus lives to make _____ for me.

  Therefore he is able to save completely those who come to God through him, because he always lives to intercede for them.

  —Hebrews 7:25

  I will remain in the world no longer, but they are still in the world, and I am coming to you. Holy Father, protect them by the power of your name —the name you gave me—so that they may be one as we are one. . . . My prayer is not that you take them out of the world but that you protect them from the evil one.

  —John 17:11, 15

- Jesus lives to _____ for me.

  My dear children, I write this to you so that you will not sin. But if anybody does sin, we have one who speaks to the Father in our defense— Jesus Christ, the Righteous One. He is the atoning sacrifice for our sins, and not only for ours but also for the sins of the whole world.

  —1 John 2:1–2

- Jesus is _____ to me even when I am not faithful to him.

  This teaching is true: If we died with him, we will also live with him. If we accept suffering, we will also rule with him. If we refuse to accept him, he will refuse to accept us. If we are not faithful, he will still be faithful, because he cannot be false to himself.

  —2 Timothy 2:11–13 (NCV)

  Let us hold unswervingly to the hope we profess, for he who promised is faithful.

  —Hebrews 10:23

A Closer Look

> We live in a day of unfaithfulness. People cannot be trusted to keep their promises. That's true of both individuals and nations. Husbands are often unfaithful to the vows they made to their wives. Wives are often unfaithful to their husbands. Children are often unfaithful to the principles taught by their parents. Parents are often unfaithful to meet the needs of their children. Employees are often unfaithful to the promises they make to their employers. And employers are often unfaithful to fulfill their obligations and responsibilities to their employees. We also have to acknowledge that Christians are often unfaithful to God, although God is never unfaithful to them. Not one of us can claim immunity from the sin of unfaithfulness.
>
> Only God is always faithful and keeps every promise in full. That fact is vital because everything we believe stands on the faithfulness of God. Our eternal destiny is at stake. In contrast to the unfaithfulness around us, it is refreshing to lift our eyes to our beloved God who is always faithful.
>
> —John MacArthur

The sealing power of the _____

In our study of the Holy Spirit, we saw that at the moment of salvation, the Holy Spirit performs several works on our behalf that secure our salvation forever.

- The Holy Spirit *regenerates* me (gives me new birth).

- The Holy Spirit *baptizes* me.

- The Holy Spirit *abides* in me as a gift from God.

- The Holy Spirit *seals* me.

> And you also were included in Christ when you heard the word of truth, the gospel of your salvation. Having believed, you were marked in him with a seal, the promised Holy Spirit.
>
> —Ephesians 1:13

We can be certain of the security of our salvation because in the past, Christ made peace with God for each of us. Today, Jesus lives to make intercession for me, and the Holy Spirit guarantees that my future is full of glory. It is God's work that makes my salvation secure—I can do nothing to make him stop loving me or stop being faithful to his own promises.

> My sheep listen to my voice; I know them, and they follow me. I give them eternal life, and they shall never perish; no one can snatch them out of my hand. My Father, who has given them to me, is greater than all; no one can snatch them out of my Father's hand.
>
> —John 10:27–29

The Personal Assurance of My Salvation

How do I handle doubts about my salvation?

Whenever a person is not sure if they are saved, there are several possibilities:

- They may not be saved.
- They may be disobeying God; disobedience causes us to lose the joy of our salvation and causes us to wonder if God still loves us.
- They may be experiencing temptation to doubt from Satan, who obviously does not want us to feel secure in our relationship with God.

What if I can't remember when I became a Christian?

Though coming to Christ is often a process, at some point, a person crosses "from death to life." No one gradually becomes "alive."

Prayer for assurance

Just pray a prayer something like this.

> *Jesus, I know I made this commitment before, but not being able to remember exactly when has caused me some real doubts. So right here and right now, on (say the date) I nail down in my heart the fact that my life is given to you. I trust in you and you alone to forgive the wrong things that I've done. I ask you to be the Lord—the leader and manager—of my life. Amen.*

If you aren't sure that you are a Christian, make sure right now. Just ask Jesus to forgive you of your sins and to come into your heart.

And when Satan tries to hassle you and cause you to wonder about whether you really are a believer, you can point to this day and remember that you *did* ask Jesus to be your Savior.

What happens to my relationship to God when I sin?

When a Christian sins, fellowship with God is broken, but the relationship remains intact. God has said that we have been adopted into his family with all the rights and privileges of his Son, Jesus. He will never disown Jesus; he'll never disown us. But sin in our lives must be dealt with. Look at these diagrams to follow the process of what happens when a Christian sins.

Sin Barriers before Salvation

Barriers on God's side		Barriers on man's side	
God	1. God's justice demands punishment of the guilty.	1. Man's knowledge of his guilt brings fear of punishment.	Man
	2. God's holiness demands rejection of the unholy.	2. Man's knowledge of his lack of holiness brings fear of rejection.	
	3. God's perfection demands devaluation of the imperfect.	3. Man's knowledge of his imperfection brings loss of self-esteem.	

Sin Barriers after Salvation When We Forget That God Totally Accepts Us

Barriers on God's side		Barriers on man's side	
God	Totally removed by Christ's death.	Expectancy of punishment, rejection, and loss of self-esteem all resulting from our early experiences with punishment.	Man

Sin Barriers after Salvation When We Have Fully Applied the Results of Christ's Atonement

Barriers on God's side		Barriers on man's side	
God	Totally removed by Christ's death.	Totally removed by the knowledge of God's total acceptance and forgiveness and by the realization that God doesn't motivate by threats of punishment, rejection, and lowered self-esteem.	Man

Effects of Sin on the Christian

What Sin Doesn't Do	What Sin Does Do
1. Bring punishment from God. 2. Make God angry with us. 3. Cause God to reject us, even temporarily. 4. Make us worthless or valueless to God. 5. Cause God to make us feel guilty.	1. Brings loving correction and discipline from God. 2. Interferes with our best personal adjustment, harms us, and eventually makes us unhappy. 3. Decreases our effectiveness in the world. 4. Damages the lives of others—especially those closest to us. 5. Brings loss of rewards in heaven. 6. Brings conviction from God.

Source: Diagrams and chart adapted from Bruce Narramore and Bill Counts, *Freedom from Guilt* (Santa Ana, Calif.: Vision House, 1974), 83–85, 93.

Are there any proofs that I am a Christian?

While God alone can see into the hearts of individuals and determine who has honestly committed themselves to him, he has told us in his Word that there are some evidences that we are to judge ourselves (not others) by:

- The _____ that God is our heavenly Father

All things have been committed to me by my Father. No one knows the Son except the Father, and no one knows the Father except the Son and those to whom the Son chooses to reveal him.

—Matthew 11:27

- A new reliance on _____

Pray all the time. Ask God for anything in line with the Holy Spirit's wishes. Plead with him, reminding him of your needs, and keep praying earnestly for all Christians everywhere.

—Ephesians 6:18 (LB)

- A new ability to understand _____

But when he, the Spirit of truth, comes, he will guide you into all truth. He will not speak on his own; he will speak only what he hears, and he will tell you what is yet to come.

—John 16:13

- A new sense of the seriousness of _____

  For the grace of God that brings salvation has appeared to all men. It teaches us to say "No" to ungodliness and worldly passions, and to live self-controlled, upright and godly lives in this present age.

  —Titus 2:11–12

- A new _____ for lost people

  Brothers, my heart's desire and prayer to God for the Israelites is that they may be saved.

  —Romans 10:1

- A new love for _____

  We know that we have passed from death to life, because we love our brothers. Anyone who does not love remains in death.

  —1 John 3:14

Key Personal Perspective

Question: Why should God allow me into his heaven?

Only answer: Because I've trusted in Christ's work on the cross

Not

  Because I'm a good person.

  Because I believe in God.

  Because I go to church.

If you can answer this question correctly, you can relinquish your doubts and fears about the security of your salvation. Begin to live in the freedom that comes from knowing your salvation is secure.

  Let us go right in, to God himself, with true hearts fully trusting him to receive us, because we have been sprinkled with Christ's blood to make us clean.

  —Hebrews 10:22 (LB)

Finish memorizing memory card 6, "The Truth about Salvation."

Appendix

Scriptures Pointing to the Security and Assurance of Our Salvation

There are an overwhelming number of Scriptures pointing to the security and assurance of our salvation. A few passages in the Bible seem to indicate that our salvation could be lost or taken from us. Here is a closer look at the meaning of those verses.

Galatians 5:4: "You who are trying to be justified by law have been alienated from Christ; you have fallen away from grace."

For many people "falling from grace" is synonymous with losing salvation. This phrase is only used once in the New Testament. The apostle Paul defends himself and the gospel of Christ against a group called the Judaizers who arrived in the city of Galatia after he left.

The Judaizers taught that salvation was found through faith in Christ as well as keeping portions of the law. The main distortion they taught concerned circumcision; they believed that the Gentile believers must be circumcised to ensure their salvation (Gal. 5:2). It was not enough to put one's trust in Christ's death as payment for sin—they taught that a man must combine his faith with works in order to gain eternal life. They also observed many of the Jewish dietary guidelines and special Feast days.

Paul was heartbroken to see the Galatian Christians so easily led astray by the Judaizers (Gal. 1:6–7). He did not fear that they were going to lose their salvation—he was concerned that they would lose the joy of their salvation by adopting a form of religion that would severely restrict their freedom (Gal. 5:1).

He warned them that trusting circumcision as a means of salvation was a waste of time (Gal. 5:2–3) because it meant they would have to try to keep the whole law again. Combining Christ and the law wouldn't work because they were two entirely different systems. Law and grace just don't mix!

Paul then uses strong language to get his point across: "You . . . have been alienated [severed or nullified] from Christ" (v. 4). By trying to integrate the law into the Gospel they were nullifying the need for Christ's death for their sin. If salvation could be attained through the law, there was no reason for Christ to die. Then he says, "You have fallen away from grace" (v. 4). To fall from grace is to abandon the salvation-by-grace model for justification and to adopt the salvation-by-works model. He wasn't threatening them with the loss of their salvation, but a loss of freedom. He knew that to "fall" from God's system of grace would lead them right back into the frustration of living under the law.

Hebrews 6:4–6 *(NASB):* "For in the case of those who have once been enlightened and have tasted of the heavenly gift and have been made partakers of the Holy Spirit, and have tasted the good word of God and the powers of the age to come, and then have fallen away, it is impossible to renew them again to repentance, since they again crucify to themselves the Son of God, and put Him to open shame."

The book of Hebrews probably was addressed to a group of Jewish Christians as indicated by the continual references to Old Testament scriptures, the theme that the old covenant was obsolete, and a concern the readers would turn away from their dependence on Christ and return to Judaism. None of these concerns would be an issue if the audience was primarily Gentile believers.

Evidently these Jewish believers were becoming disillusioned with Christianity. The writer sets out in his letter to persuade his brothers and sisters to keep the faith. These warnings are not given to people trying to make up their minds about who Christ is for the first time. They were people who at one time had expressed faith in God but were considering abandoning Christianity as a way of life.

This passage speaks of individuals who have "tasted the heavenly gift." Tasted is used in such a way as to mean "experienced," and they are said to have been "partakers" of the Holy Spirit. There's no doubt that these are genuine Christians. The author is afraid that they will return to their old ways of life, including their original form of worship (Judaism). They thought they would be returning to the God of their fathers, but actually they would be abandoning the God of their fathers.

The author used the word "repentance" in the sense of "changing one's mind." It is as though these believers have changed their minds about Christ and cannot be convinced otherwise. By turning their backs on Christ, these Jews were in essence agreeing with the Jews who had Christ arrested and put to death. Their public denial would lead outsiders to conclude that there must not be much to Christianity if those who at one time said they believed changed their minds and went back to their former religion.

This warning, though, in no way threatens the security of the believer. Instead, it is evidence for the believer's security. If a Jew, who was awaiting the coming of the Messiah, could find salvation through Christ and then walk away from him without the threat of losing his or her salvation, what do the rest of us have to fear?

Hebrews 10:26–31 (NASB): "For if we go on sinning willfully after receiving the knowledge of the truth, there no longer remains a sacrifice for sins, but a terrifying expectation of judgment, and the fury of a fire which will consume the adversaries. Anyone who has set aside the Law of Moses dies without mercy on the testimony of two or three witnesses. How much severer punishment do you think he will deserve who has trampled under foot the Son of God, and has regarded as unclean the blood of the covenant by which he was sanctified, and has insulted the Spirit of grace? For we know Him who said, 'Vengeance is Mine, I will repay.' And again, 'The Lord will judge His people.' It is a terrifying thing to fall into the hands of the living God."

If this passage teaches that willful sin results in the loss of salvation, it also teaches that salvation is lost over one willful sin. Furthermore, once it is lost, it is lost forever because there is no more sacrifice for sin.

The author of Hebrews is not writing about losing salvation. The context and details of the text rule that out as a valid interpretation.

Instead, he is warning his Jewish audience of the consequences of willful disobedience to Christ. They can no longer justify their sin in the light of the coming Messiah. He had already come. In their next encounter with the Messiah, he will stand as a Judge who will hand down decisions based on the new covenant. For believers who live for themselves with little or no thought for the things of God, it will be a "terrifying thing to fall into the hands of the living God."

Revelation 3:5 (NASB): "He who overcomes will thus be clothed in white garments; and I will not erase his name from the book of life."

These comments were directed to a group of faithful believers from the church in Sardis. Unlike the majority of people in the congregation at Sardis, these few believers had remained unsoiled by the world around them. Christ commends them for their consistent walk.

Five other times in Revelation the apostle John refers to the "book of life." In two of these passages it is clear that he did not believe that a person's name could be erased from the book of life.

Revelation 13:8 (NASB): "And all who dwell on the earth will worship him, everyone whose name has not been written from the foundation of the world in the book of life of the Lamb who has been slain."

Revelation 17:8: "The inhabitants of the earth whose names have not been written in the book of life from the creation of the world."

John is using the word "world" in Revelation 17:8 to refer to the entire universe (see John 1:3; Acts 17:24). He indicates that the book of life was filled out before the first entry was ever born. If that is the case, God's foreknowledge has a great deal to do with who was written in and who was not. In anticipation of Christ's death on man's behalf, God wrote the names of those he knew from eternity past would accept his gracious offer. God wrote before we did anything. He filled out the book of life with what he knew we would do. Therefore, he did not write in response to what we actually did; rather, he wrote in response to what he knew we would actually do.

This distinction is very important. For if God wrote in the names as history unfolded, it could be argued that he erases them as history unfolds as well. But if God entered names according to his foreknowledge, it follows that it would be complete before the world began. In that case, no one needs to live with the fear that his or her name will be erased from the book of life sometime in the future.

In other words, God's pencil has no eraser! Before you were born God knew how you would respond to his offer of grace. According to his foreknowledge, he wrote your name in the book of life. And there it shall remain forever.[2]

Discussion Questions

1. Look back at the three reasons why people lack assurance of salvation. Which one do you think most people struggle with? Has one of these been a struggle for you?

2. What is the difference between basing my sense of security in salvation on my faithfulness to God as opposed to basing it on his faithfulness to me? How does this impact our attitudes, motivations, and actions as believers?

3. What would you say to someone who said to you, "I've been attending church and praying and trying to read the Bible for years, but lately I've been feeling like I'm not really a Christian"?

4. If I believe in eternal security, where is my motivation to grow? Which of these three is the most significant for you?

- Grace

    For it is by grace you have been saved, through faith—and this not from yourselves, it is the gift of God—not by works, so that no one can boast. For we are God's workmanship, created in Christ Jesus to do good works, which God prepared in advance for us to do.

    —Ephesians 2:8–10

- Eternal rewards

    Whatever you do, work at it with all your heart, as working for the Lord, not for men.

    —Colossians 3:23

- Pleasing God

    So we make it our goal to please him, whether we are at home in the body or away from it.

    —2 Corinthians 5:9

For Further Study

Graham, Billy. *How to Be Born Again.* Dallas: Word, 1989.

Lucado, Max. *In the Grip of Grace.* Dallas: Word, 1996.

Sproul, R. C. *Faith Alone: The Evangelical Doctrine of Justification.* Grand Rapids, Mich.: Baker, 1999.

Stanley, Charles. *Eternal Security: Can You Be Sure?* Nashville: Nelson, 1990.

Strombeck, J. F. *Shall Never Perish.* Grand Rapids, Mich.: Kregel, 1991.

Swindoll, Charles R. *Grace Awakening.* Dallas: Word, 1990.

Toon, Peter. *Born Again: A Biblical and Theological Study of Regeneration.* Grand Rapids, Mich.: Baker, 1986.

White, James R. *The God Who Justifies: A Comprehensive Study on the Doctrine of Justification.* Minneapolis: Bethany House, 2001.

Answers to Fill-Ins

specific time	Spirit
correctness	knowledge
sins	prayer
Father	Scripture
Jesus	sin
intercession	love
mediate	other believers
faithful	

Sanctification

Part 1

Life Change Objectives

- To develop a deep conviction in you that, because of Jesus' love, you are holy.

- To build a foundation of truth that will lead to a lifetime of growth in Christ.

As believers we have been:

Justified

> Declared eternally not guilty (Rom. 5:1; Gal. 2:16)

Sanctified

> The act of being set apart once for all to be holy (1 Cor. 6:11)

> The experience of growing in Christlikeness (1 Thess. 5:23)

Glorified

> The completed act of our being with God for eternity (Rom. 8:30)

During the last two sessions we looked at what it means to be justified. In this study we begin a look at what it means to be sanctified.

Sanctified means _____.

In the Old Testament it was most often the places and objects of worship that were called "set apart" for God's honor and use:

Holy priests (Ex. 28:41)

Holy garments (Ex. 29:21)

A holy altar (Ex. 30:10)

The Holy Land (Lev. 27:21)

In the New Testament it is God's people who are "set apart" for God's honor and use.

> If a man cleanses himself from the latter, he will be an instrument for noble purposes, made holy, useful to the Master and prepared to do any good work.
>
> —2 Timothy 2:21

Sanctified comes from the same word as saint. In the Bible, all believers are called saints.

I am not trying to grow *toward* sainthood. I am a _____ _____ (2 Peter 3:18; 2 Cor. 10:15).

The doctrine of sanctification sets the foundation for our growth as Christians. One of the missing ingredients in our spiritual growth is an understanding of this doctrine. Without understanding the doctrine of sanctification, you can easily find yourself falling into the traps of

trying to grow in Christ based on your own effort (legalism).

presuming on God's grace to grow you no matter how you live (license).

While there are hundreds of things that we can do to grow spiritually, all rest on the foundation of faith. To grow as a Christian, you must learn to see yourself by faith—the way that God sees you. As we study sanctification, we're going to look at five specific truths about you that can be accepted only by faith. These truths form the foundation for our growth as believers.

In this session we'll look at two areas that require our faith:

1. The two focuses of sanctification
2. The two natures of the Christian

In the next session we'll cover three additional truths that require faith:

3. The power of grace over the law
4. The daily process of growth
5. God's promise to finish his work

The Two Focuses of Sanctification

Sanctification refers to two things:

The _____ of being made holy

The _____ of becoming holy

1. Sanctification is once and complete.

> And by that will, we have been made holy through the sacrifice of the body of Jesus Christ once for all.
>
> —Hebrews 10:10

Because of God you are in Christ Jesus, who has become for us wisdom from God. In Christ we are put right with God, and have been made holy, and have been set free from sin.

—1 Corinthians 1:30 (NCV)

2. Sanctification is continual and progressive.

Like newborn babies, crave pure spiritual milk, so that by it you may grow up in your salvation.

—1 Peter 2:2

Seek to live a clean and holy life, for one who is not holy will not see the Lord.

—Hebrews 12:14 (LB)

Grow in the grace and knowledge of our Lord and Savior Jesus Christ.

—2 Peter 3:18 (NCV)

One verse sums up both:

Because by one sacrifice he has made perfect forever those who are being made holy.

—Hebrews 10:14

You express faith concerning these two focuses when you say: "I am a sanctified person who is being sanctified."

This was done (finished, completed, settled) at the moment of salvation (1 Cor. 6:11; 2 Cor. 5:17).

The Two Natures of the Christian

You have both an _____ nature and a _____ nature.

A Closer Look

The Old and New Natures of the Christian

Your old nature, which the Bible also calls your "flesh," is your inner desire and tendency toward sin. It is not the feeling of being tempted; it is the inner part of who you are that inevitably will choose to say yes to various temptations. Before you became a believer, your old nature was your only nature. We all have this old nature—this natural propensity to sin—because of the fall of man that happened in the Garden of Eden.

Your new nature was given to you the moment you gave your life to Christ. The new nature is the new life and new power to live that have been given to you because of your trust in what Jesus did for you through his death and resurrection.

One of the most crucial aspects of growth in our lives as believers is learning how to trust God concerning both our old nature and our new nature.

- You express faith concerning your new nature when you see yourself as _____.

  When someone becomes a Christian, he becomes a brand new person inside. He is not the same any more. A new life has begun!
  —2 Corinthians 5:17 (LB)

1. I was "_____."

   All of us were born in sin because we are Adam's descendants. We choose to sin because that is our spiritual nature. The Bible refers to our condition as being in Adam, which means we were subject to judgment and death.

   For as in Adam all die . . .
   —1 Corinthians 15:22

2. I am now "_____."

   Spiritual life is gained only through spiritual birth (John 3:6). The moment we were born again, our soul came into union with God because of Christ. We are now in Christ.

   Praise be to the God and Father of our Lord Jesus Christ, who has blessed us in the heavenly realms with every spiritual blessing in Christ. For he chose us in him before the creation of the world to be holy and blameless in his sight.
   —Ephesians 1:3–4

   There are only two types of people in the world—those who are in Adam and those who are in Christ. You are in Christ if Christ is in you. An exchange of lives occurs: You give Jesus your life, and he gives you his.

Who Is This "New Person?"

- I am a light in the world (Matt. 5:14).
- I am a child of God (John 1:12).
- I am Christ's friend (John 15:15).
- I am chosen and appointed by Christ to bear his fruit (John 15:16).
- I am a slave of righteousness (Rom. 6:18).
- I am a joint heir with Christ (Rom. 8:17).
- I am a temple, a dwelling place, of God (1 Cor. 3:16; 6:19).
- I am a member of Christ's body (1 Cor. 12:27; Eph. 5:30).
- I am a new creation (2 Cor. 5:17).
- I am reconciled to God and a minister of reconciliation (2 Cor. 5:18–19).

- I am a saint (Eph. 1:1; 1 Cor. 2:1–2).
- I am God's workmanship (Eph. 2:10).
- I am a citizen of heaven (Phil. 3:20; Eph. 2:6).
- I am righteous and holy (Eph. 4:24).
- I am hidden with Christ in God (Col. 3:3).
- I am chosen and dearly loved (Col. 3:12).
- I am a son/daughter of light and not of darkness (1 Thess. 5:5).
- I am an enemy of the Devil (1 Peter 5:8).
- I am victorious (1 John 5:4)
- I am born again (1 Peter 1:23).
- I am alive with Christ (Eph. 2:5).
- I am more than a conqueror (Rom. 8:37).
- I am the righteousness of God (2 Cor. 5:21).
- I am born of God and the Evil One cannot touch me (1 John 5:18).
- I am to be like Christ when he returns (1 John 3:1–2).

Key Personal Perspective

Truths to Help You Live Your New Life

1. You don't have to _____ your new life.

   Newness is a creation of God.

   You have clothed yourselves with a brand-new nature that is continually being renewed as you learn more and more about Christ, who created this new nature within you.

   —Colossians 3:10 (NLT)

2. You don't have to work to _____ your new life.

   Your new life is kept with Christ in God.

   Your old sinful self has died, and your new life is kept with Christ in God.
   —Colossians 3:3 (NCV)

- You express faith concerning your old nature when you see yourself as _____.

   Your old sin-loving nature was buried with him by baptism when he died, and when God the Father, with glorious power, brought him back to life again, you were given his wonderful new life to enjoy.

   —Romans 6:4 (LB)

One of the most discussed points of doctrine over the centuries has to do with what the Bible means when it tells us that this old nature is dead. Some have suggested that this means this old nature has disappeared—which obviously is not true from our daily experience! Others suggest it is a matter of self-discipline to say no to our old nature—yet self-discipline by itself is not enough to change us.

How do we choose to trust with faith what the Bible means when it says our old sinful nature is dead?

> You were taught, with regard to your former way of life, to put off your old self, which is being corrupted by its deceitful desires.
>
> —Ephesians 4:22

How do I "put off" the old nature?

- Not by _____

- Not by _____

- By faith in what _____

> And since your old sin-loving nature "died" with Christ, we know that you will share his new life.
>
> —Romans 6:8 (LB)

 A Closer Look

Don't Miss This!

What does dead mean? (It does not mean "no longer present or an influence in your life.")

It means:

It no longer has the power to force you to sin—you have a choice.

You no longer enjoy the sin in the same way—you have changed.

- You express faith concerning your new and old natures when you see yourself with a new power to overcome evil.

Before salvation, I belonged to _____.

> You belong to your father, the devil, and you want to carry out your father's desire.
>
> —John 8:44

After salvation, I belong to _____.

And you also are among those who are called to belong to Jesus Christ.

—Romans 1:6

Because I belong to God, Satan has no power to control me.

Be self-controlled and alert. Your enemy the devil prowls around like a roaring lion looking for someone to devour. Resist him, standing firm in the faith.

—1 Peter 5:8–9

God has not left our growth to chance. The foundation of your sanctification is nothing less than the death and resurrection of Jesus Christ. This means two things:

First, because of the power of Jesus' crucifixion, you no longer have to be controlled by your old nature.

I have been crucified with Christ and I no longer live, but Christ lives in me. The life I live in the body, I live by faith in the Son of God, who loved me and gave himself for me.

—Galatians 2:20

Second, because of the power of Jesus' resurrection, you have a new nature.

In the same way, count yourselves dead to sin but alive to God in Christ Jesus. Therefore do not let sin reign in your mortal body so that you obey its evil desires. Do not offer the parts of your body to sin, as instruments of wickedness, but rather offer yourselves to God, as those who have been brought from death to life; and offer the parts of your body to him as instruments of righteousness.

—Romans 6:11–13

Begin working on memory card 7, "The Truth about Sanctification."

Discussion Questions

1. Do you think any Christian ever truly feels completely holy? Can you remember the times and places in your life when you have felt the most holy?

2. What are the inner attitudes that encourage and inspire your growth in Christ? What attitudes put up a barrier to your growth?

3. How has becoming a Christian changed your life? What new habits do you now enjoy as a Christian?

4. Have you been frustrated by the battle with sin? How do you think facing the battle through faith in God rather than with just personal willpower will make a difference in your daily life?

5. How would the truths we've talked about help you to answer someone who has the questions listed below?

   • I'm not really sure I'm a believer because of the way I sometimes act.

   • Why do I keep doing the same wrong things over and over now that I am a believer?

Answers to Fill-Ins

set apart	achieve
growing saint	keep
finished action	dead to sin
daily process	ignoring it
old	human effort
new	God has done
a new person	Satan
in Adam	God
in Christ	

Sanctification
Part 2

Life Change Objective

To decide to trust grace rather than law for your growth, God's process rather than your plan for your growth, and God's promise rather than your willpower for your growth.

In the last session we learned that sanctified means "set apart" (saint comes from the same root word).

In the Old Testament it was most often the places and objects of worship that were called "set apart" for God's honor and use:

> Holy priests (Ex. 28:41)
>
> Holy garments (Ex. 29:21)
>
> A holy altar (Ex. 30:10)
>
> The Holy Land (Lev. 27:21)

In the New Testament it is all God's people that are "set apart" for God's honor and use:

> If a man cleanses himself from the latter, he will be an instrument for noble purposes, made holy, useful to the Master and prepared to do any good work.
>
> —2 Timothy 2:21

And we looked at the first two of the five ways we put faith in God for our sanctification:

1. The two focuses of sanctification
2. The two natures of the Christian

You cannot create growth; that is God's job. But you can cooperate with the way that God grows us. In this session we're going to look at three additional ways that we have faith in what God is doing to grow us.

The Power of _____ over the _____

Just as we are justified by faith and grace, we are sanctified by faith and grace.

> You began your life in Christ by the Spirit. Now are you trying to make it complete by your own power? That is foolish.
>
> —Galatians 3:3 (NCV)

> As you received Christ Jesus the Lord, so continue to live in him.
>
> —Colossians 2:6 (NCV)

- By faith you can say, "I am _____ from the law."

The law is not dead; it is not even "bad"—as the old nature is. The law is just not capable of bringing us salvation. It can show us our sin, but it cannot make us right before God.

> Through Christ Jesus the law of the Spirit that brings life made me free from the law that brings sin and death.
>
> —Romans 8:2 (NCV)

> That old law had glory, but it really loses its glory when it is compared to the much greater glory of this new way.
>
> —2 Corinthians 3:10 (NCV)

- By faith you can say, "I have a _____!"

> Now you are free from sin, your old master, and you have become slaves to your new master, righteousness.
>
> —Romans 6:18 (NLT)

> In the past, the law held us like prisoners, but our old selves died, and we were made free from the law. So now we serve God in a new way with the Spirit, and not in the old way with written rules.
>
> —Romans 7:6 (NCV)

The _____ of Growth

- By faith you ask God to _____.

> You were taught, with regard to your former way of life, to put off your old self, which is being corrupted by its deceitful desires; to be made new in the attitude of your minds; and to put on the new self, created to be like God in true righteousness and holiness.
>
> —Ephesians 4:22–24

In the last session we looked at putting off the old and putting on the new. Being renewed in your mind is the often forgotten step in this process. Inner renewal is the key to outer transformation.

> Do not conform any longer to the pattern of this world, but be transformed by the renewing of your mind. Then you will be able to test and approve what God's will is—his good, pleasing and perfect will.
>
> —Romans 12:2

> Therefore we do not lose heart. Though outwardly we are wasting away, yet inwardly we are being renewed day by day.
>
> —2 Corinthians 4:16

Ephesians 4:25–32 helps us to see that a key aspect of this inner renewal is the ability to see God's positive reasons for making a change. A renewed mind has the ability to see things the way that God sees them. It centers on the new way of viewing the world that has been our focus in this *Foundations* study.

Put off the old self	Put on the new self	Renewed in your minds
Put off falsehood . . .	. . . speak truthfully to his neighbor . . .	. . . for we are all members of one body.
In your anger do not sin . . .	. . . do not let the sun go down while you are still angry . . .	. . . do not give the devil a foothold.
He who has been stealing must steal no longer . . .	. . . but must work . . .	. . . that he may have something to share with those in need.
Do not let any unwholesome talk come out of your mouths . . .	. . . but only what is helpful for building others up . . .	. . . do not grieve the Holy Spirit.
Get rid of all bitterness, rage and anger, brawling and slander . . .	. . . be kind and compassionate to one another, forgiving each other . . .	. . . just as in Christ God forgave you.

- By faith you practice the _____ _____.

Spend your time and energy in training yourself for spiritual fitness.

—1 Timothy 4:7 (NLT)

Discipline yourself for the purpose of godliness.

—1 Timothy 4:7 (NASB)

A Closer Look

Three of the most important disciplines of growth through which God sanctifies us are:

1. A daily quiet time—in God's Word and prayer

   Jesus answered, "It is written: 'Man does not live on bread alone, but on every word that comes from the mouth of God.'"

   —Matthew 4:4

   Sanctify them by the truth; your word is truth.

   —John 17:17

2. A weekly tithe to God

   "Bring the whole tithe into the storehouse, that there may be food in my house. Test me in this," says the LORD Almighty, "and see if I will not throw open the floodgates of heaven and pour out so much blessing that you will not have room enough for it."

   —Malachi 3:10

   And they gave in a way we did not expect: They first gave themselves to the Lord and to us. This is what God wants.

   —2 Corinthians 8:5 (NCV)

3. A regular commitment to a small group

   So now you Gentiles are no longer strangers and foreigners. You are citizens along with all of God's holy people. You are members of God's family.

   —Ephesians 2:19 (NLT)

- By faith you choose to trust God in the _____ _____.

God has allowed our choice to be one of the key factors in our growth. One of the most important choices we make is our response to the difficulties and trials we all face as a part of life.

Dear brothers, is your life full of difficulties and temptations? Then be happy, for when the way is rough, your patience has a chance to grow. So let it grow, and don't try to squirm out of your problems. For when your patience is finally in full bloom, then you will be ready for anything, strong in character, full and complete.

—James 1:2–4 (LB)

We also have joy with our troubles, because we know that these troubles produce patience. And patience produces character, and character produces hope. And this hope will never disappoint us, because God has poured out his love to fill our hearts. He gave us his love through the Holy Spirit, whom God has given to us.

—Romans 5:3–5 (NCV)

So even though Jesus was God's Son, he learned obedience from the things he suffered.

—Hebrews 5:8 (NLT)

God's Promise to _____

What is the ultimate goal that God is working toward in your life?

The goal is to be like Christ.

> We know that in everything God works for the good of those who love him. They are the people he called, because that was his plan. God knew them before he made the world, and he decided that they would be like his Son so that Jesus would be the firstborn of many brothers.
>
> —Romans 8:28–29 (NCV)

> We know that when Christ comes again, we will be like him, because we will see him as he really is.
>
> —1 John 3:2 (NCV)

> This work must continue until we are all joined together in the same faith and in the same knowledge of the Son of God. We must become like a mature person, growing until we become like Christ and have his perfection.
>
> —Ephesians 4:13 (NCV)

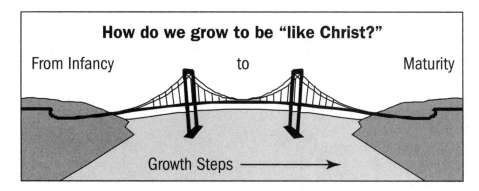

- By faith you believe in God's ability to accomplish his work in your life.

  You are not alone. God is working for your growth. He is working to make you like his Son, Jesus.

  God is _____ to your growth.

> And I consecrate myself to meet their need for growth in truth and holiness.
>
> —John 17:19 (LB)

> Long ago, even before he made the world, God chose us to be his very own, through what Christ would do for us; he decided then to make us holy in his eyes, without a single fault—we who stand before him covered with his love.
>
> —Ephesians 1:4 (LB)

Our motivational power: God _____ us and is _____ for us to be sanctified.

> He who began a good work in you will carry it on to completion until the day of Christ Jesus.
>
> —Philippians 1:6

Key Personal Perspective

Growth is not accomplished by _____, but by _____.

Trust means: We work out what God works in.

> Continue to work out your salvation with fear and trembling, for it is God who works in you to will and to act according to his good purpose.
>
> —Philippians 2:12–13

> And now—all glory to him who alone is God, who saves us through Jesus Christ our Lord; yes, splendor and majesty, all power and authority are his from the beginning; his they are and his they evermore shall be. And he is able to keep you from slipping and falling away, and to bring you, sinless and perfect, into his glorious presence with mighty shouts of everlasting joy. Amen.
>
> —Jude 1:24–25 (LB)

Finish memorizing memory card 7, "The Truth about Sanctification."

Discussion Questions

1. Why do you think some get pulled into thinking we can measure our spiritual growth based solely on how we keep laws or rules?

2. What are two or three practical things that we can do to cooperate with God in his desire to renew our minds?

3. Which of the disciplines of growth do you find God using the most frequently and/or the most effectively in your life?

4. The goal of becoming completely like Christ will never be fully realized by any of us while on this earth. What are the practical and personal ways that you keep from getting discouraged as you reach for a goal you won't reach until you get to heaven?

For Further Study

Bridges, Jerry. *The Practice of Godliness.* Colorado Springs: NavPress, 1983.

Cloud, Henry and John Townsend. *How People Grow.* Grand Rapids, Mich.: Zondervan, 2001.

Dieter, Melvin E., et al. *Five Views on Sanctification.* Grand Rapids, Mich.: Zondervan, 1987.

Foster, Richard J. *Celebration of Discipline.* Rev. ed. San Francisco: Harper & Row, 1988.

Henrichsen, Walter A. *Disciples Are Made—Not Born.* Wheaton, Ill.: Victor, 1980.

Nouwen, Henri J. M. *Reaching Out: The Three Movements of the Spiritual Life.* New York: Doubleday, 1986.

Ortberg, John. *The Life You've Always Wanted.* Grand Rapids, Mich.: Zondervan, 1997.

Willard, Dallas. *The Spirit of the Disciplines.* San Francisco: HarperSanFrancisco, 1991.

Answers to Fill-Ins

grace	circumstances of life
law	finish his work
free	committed
new master	wants
daily process	working
renew your mind	trying hard
disciplines of growth	trusting him

Good and Evil
Part 1

Life Change Objective

To give you the truth you need to answer questions concerning the fact that we live in an evil world.

During these next two sessions we'll be looking at what the Bible says about the fact that good and evil exist alongside each other in the world today. There are many questions that are answered by understanding God's perspective on this truth:

- How could God allow such things as war and the death of children in the world today?
- If God is all-powerful and all-loving, why can't he stop evil?
- Why do bad things happen to good people?
- In light of what's happening in the world, am I just fooling myself to think that there is any hope?
- Will it ever end? When?

First we'll look at the overall problem of good and evil. Why does it exist in this world?

Next we'll look at the personal side of good and evil. How do I win the battle against evil in my personal life?

Why Does Evil Exist in God's World?

Three truths

1. God is good.

   His _____ is good.

   For the LORD is good and his love endures forever; his faithfulness continues through all generations.

   —Psalm 100:5

   His _____ are good.

   God saw all that he had made, and it was very good.

   —Genesis 1:31

2. God is all-powerful.

> Great and powerful God, your name is the LORD All-Powerful.
>
> —Jeremiah 32:18 (NCV)

3. The world is evil.

> Their sentence is based on this fact: that the Light from heaven came into the world, but they loved the darkness more than the Light, for their deeds were evil.
>
> —John 3:19 (LB)

> Stop loving this evil world and all that it offers you.
>
> —1 John 2:15 (LB)

How can all of these be true?

How could a good and all-powerful God create a world in which evil could exist and continues to exist? A lot of theological and philosophical jargon can be summed up in one simple sentence:

There is no _____ without _____.

God could have made a person who would never have chosen to sin, but then that person would have been denied the opportunity to choose to love.

 A Closer Look

Two Truths to Remember

1. God is sovereign.
2. Mankind has free choice.

How do you reconcile those two? If God gives us choice, doesn't that put us in control rather than him? Our God is an awesome God! He is able to give us, as a part of his creation, a free will to decide and yet remain in complete control of his creation. How does he do that? He is God!

One warning: be sure to keep these truths in balance. If you lean too far toward God's being in control, you come down on the side of fatalism: it doesn't matter what we do. If you lean too far toward man's free will, you come down on the side of humanism: we are in control of our fate.

There are three reasons that evil exists in our world today.

God's Will: Because God _____

Evil

The problem of evil and suffering is possibly the single greatest intellectual challenge to Christianity. It's hard for people to understand how a great and good God could allow evil to exist.

1. He made a world in which evil _____.

   In Genesis 3:

   • God planted the tree of the knowledge of good and evil.

   • God let Satan as a snake into the garden.

   • God allowed Adam and Eve to eat of the fruit.

2. God allows evil to _____.

   • God allows us to make evil choices.

     So I gave them over to their stubborn hearts to follow their own devices.

     —Psalm 81:12

   • God allows painful consequences for the evil choices we make.

     If someone sins and without realizing it does one of the things forbidden by Yahweh's commandments, he will answer for it and bear the consequences of his guilt.

     —Leviticus 5:17 (NJB)

A Closer Look

God's Response to Suffering

The fact that God allows suffering does not mean he enjoys suffering.

1. He directly _____ some suffering. He is the punisher of evil (Isa. 13:11).

2. He has _____ for all suffering (2 Cor. 1:3–4; Lam. 3:22–23; Matt. 14:14).

3. He is willing to _____ for us in our suffering (Ps. 46:1; Heb. 4:16).

4. He develops our _____ through suffering (James 1:2–4; Heb. 2:10).

5. He will one day _____ all suffering (Rev. 21:3–4; Rom. 8:18).

Satan's Influence:
Because Satan _____ Evil

The influence of Satan is a second reason why evil exists in our world today. Evil is not some new creation of Satan—Satan does not have the power to create anything. All he can do is to try to twist or to withhold what God has created.

Is weather evil?

Is ambition evil?

Is sex evil?

Is our ability to talk evil?

All of these are good creations of God. Evil is when Satan twists them into natural disasters, or war, or immorality, or slander.

We as believers need to be able to understand and defeat the enemy without glorifying the enemy. Satan has power, but he is also stupid. (Why else would he have sinned against God?)

Satan: a brief biography

Many of the ideas and pictures of Satan that we grew up with were influenced more by English literature such as Dante's *Inferno* and Milton's *Paradise Lost* than by the Bible. Here we're going to look at the straight story from the Bible about who Satan is.

1. He was an _____ in heaven (Rev. 12:3–9; 9:11).

2. He _____ from heaven due to pride.

> And there was war in heaven. Michael and his angels fought against the dragon, and the dragon and his angels fought back. But he was not strong enough, and they lost their place in heaven. The great dragon was hurled down—that ancient serpent called the devil, or Satan, who leads the whole world astray. He was hurled to the earth, and his angels with him.
> —Revelation 12:7–9

> How you are fallen from heaven, O Lucifer, son of the morning! How you are cut down to the ground—mighty though you were against the nations of the world. For you said to yourself, "I will ascend to heaven and rule the angels. I will take the highest throne. I will preside on the Mount of Assembly far away in the north. I will climb to the highest heavens and be like the Most High." But instead, you will be brought down to the pit of hell, down to its lowest depths.
> —Isaiah 14:12–15 (LB)

3. He has been given _____ freedom to influence the earth.

   Satan's limit: he must ask _____.

   Some examples:
   - Job (Job 1:6–12; 2:1–6)
   - Peter: "Satan has asked to sift you as wheat" (Luke 22:31).

4. He is unalterably _____ to eternal destruction.

Satan will be thrown into the lake of fire, to be tormented forever.

> And the devil, who deceived them, was thrown into the lake of burning sulfur.
>
> —Revelation 20:10

Mankind's Choice: Because We _____ Evil

Remember two truths:

1. Evil began with _____ (Gen. 3).

   The choice that Adam and Eve made to sin had horrible consequences:

   - If they ate of the tree they would "surely die." Sin brings death: spiritual and physical death.

     > But you must not eat from the tree of the knowledge of good and evil, for when you eat of it you will surely die.
     >
     > —Genesis 2:17

   - Because they ate from the tree, they were banished from the Garden of Eden. Sin causes us to live in a fallen, imperfect world.

     > So the LORD God banished him from the Garden of Eden to work the ground from which he had been taken.
     >
     > —Genesis 3:23

   - Adam and Eve passed along to us as their children a sin nature. Sin became a part of all of us when they bit into that fruit. That's why we all inevitably sin. We cannot refuse the temptation of evil.

     This is called "original sin." We don't start with a clean slate. We all start with the knowledge of good and of evil and with a flawed heart that causes us to sin.

     > Therefore, just as sin entered the world through one man, and death through sin, and in this way death came to all men, because all sinned.
     >
     > —Romans 5:12

2. Evil is present in _____.

   It's not just "their fault." We need to be able to admit that "evil is present in me."

   > When I want to do good, evil is right there with me.
   >
   > —Romans 7:21

153

What shall we conclude then? Are we any better? Not at all! We have already made the charge that Jews and Gentiles alike are all under sin. As it is written: "There is no one righteous, not even one; there is no one who understands, no one who seeks God. All have turned away, they have together become worthless; there is no one who does good, not even one."

—Romans 3:9–12

The line separating good and evil passes not through states, nor between classes, nor between political parties—but right through every human heart.[1]

The Questions That Remain

Why does God continue to allow evil? Why doesn't God stop it?

1. He already has defeated evil (1 Cor. 15:57; Col. 2:15).

   He defeated evil at the cross and will allow us to join him in that victory for all eternity. We are fighting a battle in which ultimate victory is assured.

2. He is _____.

   God has provided for the salvation of all (1 John 2:2).

   God desires for all to be saved (1 Tim. 2:3–4).

   And he waits patiently, desiring all to come to salvation (2 Peter 3:9).

Key Personal Perspective

How do you answer someone when they ask you a question like: "How could a perfect, good, and all-powerful God allow wars and disease in the world today?" When faced with tragedy our first impulse is to ask, "Why? Why would God allow this to happen?" The study has reminded us of some of the answers, for ourselves and for others.

1. The world is evil, not because of God's creation, but because of mankind's _____.

2. God _____ about those who suffer.

3. It is God's proclaimed purpose to one day do away with evil.

4. The reason he waits is so that more people might be _____, therefore not having to suffer eternal separation from him.

Begin working on memory card 8, "The Truth about Good and Evil."

Discussion Questions

1. Why do you think it's important that we be honest about the fact that we live in an evil world? What happens when we live in denial of the reality of evil?

2. Why do you think it was so important for God to give us free choice?

3. What is the difference between God allowing evil and God doing evil?

4. What is the thing that gives you the greatest hope and encouragement as you face personal suffering?

5. What has helped you to replace your fears of Satan and evil with faith in God?

6. Why is it unhealthy to always blame others for the evil in the world?

7. Jesus taught us to pray "deliver us from evil" (Matt. 6:13 NASB). In what circumstance would you like others to pray for you to be delivered from evil?

Answers to Fill-Ins

character	angel
actions	fell
love, choice	limited
allows	God's permission
could exist	condemned
continue to exist	accept
causes	them
compassion	me
care	patient
character	choice
cease	cares
afflicts	saved

Good and Evil
Part 2

Life Change Objective

To enable you to live with victory over evil and Satan:

In one specific thought

In one specific habit

In one specific relationship

In one specific problem

Key Personal Perspective

You are victorious over Satan!

> Everyone who is a child of God conquers the world. And this is the victory that conquers the world—our faith.
>
> —1 John 5:4 (NCV)

> God stripped the spiritual rulers and powers of their authority. With the cross, he won the victory and showed the world that they were powerless.
>
> —Colossians 2:15 (NCV)

> But we thank God! He gives us the victory through our Lord Jesus Christ.
> —1 Corinthians 15:57 (NCV)

> Overwhelming victory is ours through Christ who loved us enough to die for us.
>
> —Romans 8:37 (LB)

In the last session we looked at the overall problem of evil. In this session we will focus on the personal battle that we all have with evil. As you see from the verses above, God has guaranteed us victory, but it does not come without a struggle. In this study we're going to look at how to win the battle with evil in your daily life.

Set Your Mind on Victory

Be _____

The Bible gives us two powerful pictures to help us to be alert and aware:

1. We live "_____."

   We know that we belong to God even though the whole world is under the rule of the Evil One.

   —1 John 5:19 (GNT)

2. Satan is a "_____."

   Be self-controlled and alert. Your enemy the devil prowls around like a roaring lion looking for someone to devour.

   —1 Peter 5:8

Be _____

"God opposes the proud but gives grace to the humble." Submit yourselves, then, to God. Resist the devil, and he will flee from you.

   —James 4:6–7

In every case, you start resisting Satan by _____ to God.

Be _____

- Confident because of God's presence

  The one who is in you is greater than the one who is in the world.

  —1 John 4:4

- Confident because of God's promise

  The God of peace will soon crush Satan under your feet. The grace of our Lord Jesus be with you.

  —Romans 16:20

- Confident because of your prayers

  Jesus told us to pray with faith for personal victory over evil.

  Lead us not into temptation, but deliver us from the evil one.

  —Matthew 6:13

Understand the Three Channels of Evil

While Satan is the source of all evil, there are three different channels, or pipelines, through which evil has an opportunity to influence us as individuals. To live with victory, you must understand what these channels are and must know the biblical strategy for victory.

The _____

Know your enemy

In any battle, one of the keys to victory over an enemy is knowing and understanding that enemy.

The world means the philosophy and influence that reigns on this earth.

> For everything in the world—the cravings of sinful man, the lust of his eyes and the boasting of what he has and does—comes not from the Father but from the world.
>
> —1 John 2:16

Strategy for victory

What is the personal choice that I can make to begin to enjoy victory on this particular battleground?

_____ the Lord.

> Do not love the world or anything in the world. If anyone loves the world, the love of the Father is not in him. For everything in the world—the cravings of sinful man, the lust of his eyes and the boasting of what he has and does—comes not from the Father but from the world. The world and its desires pass away, but the man who does the will of God lives forever.
>
> —1 John 2:15–17

The _____

Know your enemy

A Fresh Word

Two meanings for flesh in the Bible:

1. Our physical bodies (1 Cor. 15:39; John 1:14)
2. Our spiritual "disposition to sin" (1 Cor. 3:3 NASB)

This is important stuff! There is a huge difference between saying, "Our bodies are evil" and "Our flesh is evil."

Remember our study of the Holy Spirit? Our bodies are meant to be temples of the Holy Spirit! First Corinthians 15 tells us that our bodies will one day be resurrected to eternal life. Sin starts in our unwilling hearts, not our physical bodies. Sin comes from the inside out rather than outside in. The heart is where the evil is. We don't think evil things because we live in an evil world; we live in an evil world because we think evil things (Matt. 15:10–20)!

Strategy for victory

You, my brothers, were called to be free. But do not use your freedom to indulge the sinful nature; rather, serve one another in love. . . . So I say, live by the Spirit, and you will not gratify the desires of the sinful nature.

—Galatians 5:13, 16

_____ one another in love.

_____ by the Spirit.

The Devil

Know your enemy

See the last session's study.

Strategy for victory

Put on spiritual _____.

Therefore put on the full armor of God, so that when the day of evil comes, you may be able to stand your ground, and after you have done everything, to stand. Stand firm then, with the belt of truth buckled around your waist, with the breastplate of righteousness in place, and with your feet fitted with the readiness that comes from the gospel of peace. In addition to all this, take up the shield of faith, with which you can extinguish all the flaming arrows of the evil one. Take the helmet of salvation and the sword of the Spirit, which is the word of God. And pray in the Spirit on all occasions with all kinds of prayers and requests. With this in mind, be alert and always keep on praying for all the saints.

—Ephesians 6:13–18

What is this armor? Don't focus so much on the picture of belts and breastplates in Ephesians 6; focus on what the picture is communicating. Paul discusses seven things that are armor against the Devil's schemes:

1. Truth
2. Righteousness
3. Readiness to share the Good News
4. Faith
5. Salvation
6. God's Word
7. Prayer

Overcome Evil in My Daily Life

There are many ways that we must face the reality of evil in the choices and circumstances of our daily lives. How do I enjoy God's victory when I face these different types of evil in my life?

Sin

We face evil because of our personal choice to sin.

> Jesus replied, "I tell you the truth, everyone who sins is a slave to sin."
>
> —John 8:34

Want victory? Decide to _____.

> But if we confess our sins to God, he will keep his promise and do what is right: he will forgive us our sins and purify us from all our wrongdoing.
>
> —1 John 1:9 (TEV)

> Repent, therefore, and return, in order that times of refreshing may come from the presence of the Lord.
>
> —Acts 3:19

Trials

We face evil because we live in this fallen world. And we face the painful circumstances that are an inevitable part of living in this fallen world. We can bring those trials on ourselves, but they sometimes come through no fault of our own.

> God whispers to us in our pleasures,
> speaks in our conscience,
> but shouts in our pains:
> it is His megaphone to rouse a deaf world.[1]
>
> —C. S. Lewis

Want victory? Decide to _____ (Matt. 5:12; Rom. 5:3–4).

> James, a servant of God and of the Lord Jesus Christ, To the twelve tribes scattered among the nations: Greetings. Consider it pure joy, my brothers, whenever you face trials of many kinds, because you know that the testing of your faith develops perseverance. Perseverance must finish its work so that you may be mature and complete, not lacking anything.
>
> —James 1:1–4

Key Personal Perspective

Two reasons God allows problems in our lives:

1. To develop maturity (James 1:1–4; Rom. 5:3–4).
   God can bring ultimate good out of temporary evil (Gen. 50:20; Rom. 8:28).

2. To enable _____ (2 Cor. 1:3–7 LB).

Temptation

We face evil because Satan tempts us to do wrong.

Want victory? Decide to _____ (Luke 22:46; Luke 4:1–13).

Four truths to remember about temptation:

1. Temptation will always be a part of our lives (Luke 4:2; 1 Thess. 3:5).

   Jesus was perfect, and he was tempted.

2. It is not a sin to be tempted; it's a sin to give in to the temptation.

   Jesus was tempted, but he never sinned (Matt. 4:1; Heb. 4:15).

3. We all face the same temptations.

   > When the woman saw that the fruit of the tree was good for food and pleasing to the eye, and also desirable for gaining wisdom, she took some and ate it. She also gave some to her husband, who was with her, and he ate it.
   >
   > —Genesis 3:6

   > These are the ways of the world: wanting to please our sinful selves, wanting the sinful things we see, and being too proud of what we have. None of these come from the Father, but all of them come from the world.
   >
   > —1 John 2:16 (NCV)

4. There is _____ a way of escape.

   > No temptation has seized you except what is common to man. And God is faithful; he will not let you be tempted beyond what you can bear. But when you are tempted, he will also provide a way out so that you can stand up under it.
   >
   > —1 Corinthians 10:13

 A Closer Look

An Often Asked Question

How do you deal with a "habitual sin"—the cycle of sin, confess, sin, confess?

Change the pattern to "sin—confess—*refocus.*"

Sometimes we become our own worst enemy. The more we focus on what we're *not* going to do, the more we're tempted by it and drawn into doing it. If you get into a tug-of-war with Satan, you'll lose! The solution: Drop your end of the rope and walk away. Refuse to play Satan's game.

Here are four ways to refocus your thinking.

1. Worship.
2. Radical departure (Matt. 5:29–30).
3. Tell the truth; accountability with another person.
4. Faithfulness over time.

Don't be discouraged if you do not feel an immediate change. Think of it as balancing a scale. As you continue to put weight on the positive side, one day the scales will tip.

The Number 1 Principle for Overcoming Evil

Take the offensive!

- When faced with inner accusation, picture the _____.

  God took away Satan's power to accuse you of sin, and God openly displayed to the whole world Christ's triumph at the cross where your sins were all taken away.

  —Colossians 2:15 (LB)

- When faced with outer confrontation, picture yourself as _____.

  The Lord will rescue me from every evil attack and will bring me safely to his heavenly kingdom. To him be glory for ever and ever. Amen.

  —2 Timothy 4:18

  [He] gave himself for our sins to rescue us from the present evil age.

  —Galatians 1:4

- When faced with evil, do _____.

  Do not be overcome by evil, but overcome evil with good.

  —Romans 12:21

This extremely significant verse tells us how important our focus is. You'll never defeat evil by focusing on evil: Satan and demons and the evil forces of this world. Evil is defeated by focusing on what is good and living what is good.

  We come through all these things triumphantly victorious, by the power of him who loved us.

  —Romans 8:37 (NJB)

**Acting
on the Truth**

How can you overcome evil with good this week?

In one specific thought: how can you change your focus from what is evil to what is good in the way that you're thinking?

In one specific habit: how can you change a bad habit by instead committing to a good habit?

In one specific relationship: how can you begin to see what someone might have meant for evil as something that God can use for good?

In one specific problem: how can you rejoice in what God is doing in your life through a problem you're facing right now?

Finish memorizing memory card 8, "The Truth about Good and Evil."

Discussion Questions

1. In what ways do you see God reminding you to put your confidence in him and not in yourself? Do any examples come to mind of how your confidence in Christ has been strengthened?

2. Through which "channel" does evil seem to exert its influence on you more often: the world, the flesh, or the Devil? Why do you think that is?

3. Which of the seven pieces of armor listed in Ephesians 6 have you found to be the most effective in giving you protection from evil? How do you put on this armor in your daily life?

4. What have you found to be the most effective way for you to deal with personal temptation? Do you struggle most with overcoming pride, pleasure, or possession (the temptation to be, to do, or to have)?

5. Talk together about how you would answer the four questions about our thoughts, habits, relationships, and problems in Acting on the Truth at the end of this study. Ask your group to pray for you in one of these areas this next week.

For Further Study

Elwell, Walter, ed. *Topical Analysis of the Bible.* Grand Rapids, Mich.: Baker, 1991.

Geisler, Norman, and Ron Brooks. *When Skeptics Ask.* Wheaton, Ill.: Victor, 1990.

Lewis, C. S. *The Problem of Pain.* New York: Touchstone, 1996.

Little, Paul. *Know What You Believe.* Wheaton, Ill.: Victor, 1987.

Rhodes, Ron. *The Heart of Christianity.* Eugene, Ore.: Harvest House, 1996.

Yancey, Philip. *Disappointment with God.* Grand Rapids, Mich.: Zondervan, 1988.

Yancey, Philip. *Where Is God When It Hurts?* Grand Rapids, Mich.: Zondervan, 1990.

Answers to Fill-Ins

alert	live
behind enemy lines	armor
roaring lion	repent
humble	rejoice
submitting	ministry
confident	reject
world	always
love	cross
flesh	rescued
serve	good

The Afterlife
Part 1

Life Change Objectives

- To give you a deep understanding and gratitude for God's rescue from the certainty of an eternity without him.

- To change the way you think about yourself and others: from a focus on the here and now to a focus on eternity.

All of us wonder about the end of our lives: how much time we have left, under what circumstances we will die, and just exactly what death will be like. The Bible gives us some clear truths about the end of our lives that we all need to understand. These truths affect the way we live today and the way we see the future.

In this session we'll look at what the Bible says about hell. We'll cover heaven in the next session (bad news first, then end on the good news!).

The most frequently asked questions about hell include:

Is there really a literal hell?

Why was hell created?

Who will be in hell?

What happens to people in hell?

Where do people go *now* when they die?

How can I be sure that I won't go to hell?

Is Hell a Real Place?

Jesus taught that hell is a real place of judgment. (In fact, there are more verses in which he taught about hell than about heaven.)

> Then they will go away to eternal punishment, but the righteous to eternal life.
>
> —Matthew 25:46

> Most assuredly, I say to you, he who hears My word and believes in Him who sent Me has everlasting life, and shall not come into judgment, but has passed from death into life . . . for the hour is coming in which all who are in the graves will hear His voice and come forth—those who have done good, to the resurrection of life, and those who have done evil, to the resurrection of condemnation.
>
> —John 5:24, 28–29 (NKJV)

The Bible speaks of a time of judgment that all human beings will have to go through. It is referred to in several verses as being a time of "separating" or "sorting" the righteous from the unrighteous.

Verse	Metaphor
Matthew 13:47–51	A dragnet catching fish
Matthew 25:31–46	Shepherd sorting sheep and goats
Matthew 13:24–30	Harvester pulling weeds and wheat

Who is the one who judges and does the separating? _____, the only righteous one.

> For he has set a day for justly judging the world by the man he has appointed, and has pointed him out by bringing him back to life again.
>
> —Acts 17:31 (LB)

Why Was Hell Created?

- Hell was not created originally for any human being, but for

  _____.

> Then he will say to those on his left, "Depart from me, you who are cursed, into the eternal fire prepared for the devil and his angels."
>
> —Matthew 25:41

These are the angels who followed Satan when he tried to lead a rebellion against God in heaven. They are also called demons.

- Contrary to popular opinion, Satan is not yet confined to hell. He now resides _____.

Four times in the Gospels, Jesus called Satan the "prince of this world."

> Now is the time for judgment on this world; now the prince of this world will be driven out.
>
> —John 12:31

- One day (according to the book of Revelation), God is going to cast Satan, death, and Hades into the _____ (another name for hell).

  And the devil, who deceived them, was thrown into the lake of burning sulfur, where the beast and the false prophet had been thrown. They will be tormented day and night for ever and ever.
  —Revelation 20:10

  Then death and Hades were thrown into the lake of fire. The lake of fire is the second death.
  —Revelation 20:14

Who Will Be in Hell?

Hell was created for Satan and the demons, but they, sadly, will not be the only ones in hell for eternity.

The facts of life and eternity that we must all eventually face are:

- We were all headed for an eternity without God in hell.

  All have sinned and are not good enough for God's glory.
  —Romans 3:23 (NCV)

- Jesus came to rescue us from this certainty of separation from God.

  He is the one who has rescued us from the terrors of the coming judgment.
  —1 Thessalonians 1:10 (NLT)

  Only Jesus can rescue us because only he can offer us forgiveness for the sin that is the reason we would spend eternity in hell.

- Those who trust Jesus *are* rescued!

  Therefore he is able, once and forever, to save everyone who comes to God through him. He lives forever to plead with God on their behalf.
  —Hebrews 7:25 (NLT)

- Those who do not trust Jesus are *not* rescued from hell and separation from God.

  And this is the testimony: God has given us eternal life, and this life is in his Son. He who has the Son has life; he who does not have the Son of God does not have life.
  —1 John 5:11–12

Key Personal Perspective

What about the people I love?

After we ourselves have been rescued from hell by trusting in the grace and love of Jesus, our minds immediately turn to those we love. The thought of their spending eternity separated from God is almost too painful for us to bear.

If they're still living, _____!

Let those you love know the Good News that God can rescue them too. Many who initially reject God's invitation to life and forgiveness through Jesus end up accepting him. (The apostle Paul was one of those.)

If they've already died, _____.

Remember that God is the ultimate judge of eternity; you are not. Instead of getting caught up in worrying about changing what you cannot change, leave it with God. Let your concern motivate you to share with those who are still living the hope that Jesus gives. And make sure that those you love have no doubt about your faith in Christ and the fact that you know you are going to heaven when you die.

What Happens to People in Hell?

The Bible clearly teaches that hell is a place of never-ending torment, torture, and anguish.

> Then they will go away to eternal punishment, but the righteous to eternal life.
>
> —Matthew 25:46

Emotional/relational torment

> But the subjects of the kingdom will be thrown outside, into the darkness, where there will be weeping and gnashing of teeth.
>
> —Matthew 8:12

> Do not be afraid of those who kill the body but cannot kill the soul; rather be afraid of God, who can destroy both body and soul in hell.
>
> —Matthew 10:28 (GNT)

Physical torment

So if your hand makes you lose your faith, cut it off! It is better for you to enter life without a hand than to keep both hands and go off to hell, to the fire that never goes out. And if your foot makes you lose your faith, cut if off! It is better for you to enter life without a foot than to keep both feet and be thrown into hell. And if your eye makes you lose your faith, take it out! It is better for you to enter the Kingdom of God with only one eye than to keep both eyes and be thrown into hell. There "the worms that eat them never die, and the fire that burns them is never put out."

—Mark 9:43–48 (GNT)

Spiritual torment

Then he will say to those on his left, "Depart from me, you who are cursed, into the eternal fire prepared for the devil and his angels."

—Matthew 25:41

They will be punished with everlasting destruction and shut out from the presence of the Lord and from the majesty of his power.

—2 Thessalonians 1:9

Where Do People Go Now When They Die?

According to New Testament teaching, believers go immediately into the presence of God to await resurrection of the body and the eternal joy of heaven. Unbelievers go to Hades for punishment and to await the resurrection of the body and final punishment in hell.

This simple statement brings up a *lot* of questions! These include the growth in New Testament and Old Testament teaching concerning the afterlife, the intermediate state between now and Jesus' final judgment, and the future resurrection of the body. Because a great deal of false teaching and unfounded fears grow out of a misunderstanding of these truths, we'll take an in-depth look at them.

The progressive revelation of the afterlife in the Bible

1. In much of the Old Testament, the afterlife was seen as shadowy and unknown.

Sheol

The Hebrew word *Sheol* is used sixty-six times in the Old Testament. The Old Testament consistently refers to the body as going to the grave, and the soul of man as going to Sheol. The earliest thought of Sheol indicates there was no distinction made in the minds of people between the morally good and the bad; all went to Sheol (Gen. 25:8; 37:35). As time went on, people began to believe that Sheol had sections; there is a contrast between the "lowest part" and the "highest part." While not clearly stated, it seems like the wicked are in the lowest part, while the righteous are in the highest part (Deut. 32:22).

 ### A Closer Look

While the Old Testament saints did not have a clear and precise understanding of what happens after death, this lack of understanding did not keep them from enjoying eternal rewards. They may not have known they were going into God's presence, but they certainly did go there.

---

2. During the intertestamental period (the 400 years between the final events of the Old Testament and the first events of the New Testament) the Jewish concept of Sheol had progressed to the stage where it was believed that Sheol had two distinct compartments.

   One section was a place of torment for the wicked, called

   _____.

   The other was a place of conscious bliss, often called

   _____ or _____.

   Now there was a rich man, and he habitually dressed in purple and fine linen, joyously living in splendor every day. And a poor man named Lazarus was laid at his gate, covered with sores, and longing to be fed with the crumbs which were falling from the rich man's table; besides, even the dogs were coming and licking his sores. Now the poor man died and was carried away by the angels to Abraham's bosom; and the rich man also died and was buried. In Hades he lifted up his eyes, being in torment, and saw Abraham far away and Lazarus in his bosom. And he cried out and said, "Father Abraham, have mercy on me, and send Lazarus so that he may dip the tip of his finger in water and cool off my tongue, for I am in agony in this flame." But Abraham said, "Child, remember that during your life you received your good things, and likewise Lazarus bad things; but now he is being comforted here, and you are in agony. And besides all this, between us and you there is a great chasm fixed, so that those who wish to come over from here to you will not be able, and that none may cross over from there to us." And he said, "Then I beg you, father, that you send him to my father's house—for I have five brothers—in order that he may warn them, so that they will not also come to this place of torment." But Abraham said, "They have Moses and the Prophets; let them hear them." But he said, "No, father Abraham, but if someone goes to them from the dead, they will repent!" But he said to him, "If they do not listen to Moses and the Prophets, they will not be persuaded even if someone rises from the dead."

—Luke 16:19–31 (NASB)

A Closer Look

Jesus' story in Luke 16 teaches us two hard-to-hear truths:

1. There is _____ from torment.

2. There are no _____.

3. After Christ's resurrection, the New Testament teaches that believers who die enter immediately into the presence of Christ and that unbelievers enter immediately into a place of punishment and separation from God.

I am torn between the two: I desire to depart and be with Christ.

—Philippians 1:23

The intermediate state and the resurrection of the body

Therefore we are always confident and know that as long as we are at home in the body we are away from the Lord. We live by faith, not by sight. We are confident, I say, and would prefer to be away from the body and at home with the Lord.

—2 Corinthians 5:6–8

The "intermediate state" is the phrase used by theologians to describe the state that those who die are in between now and the time that Jesus comes again.

Why the difference? Because while our souls go immediately to be with God or to suffer in Hades, our bodies have not yet been resurrected as Jesus' body was resurrected.

They found the stone rolled away from the tomb, but when they entered, they did not find the body of the Lord Jesus.

—Luke 24:2–3

The Bible tells us clearly that:

- When Jesus was resurrected he had a resurrected body (John 20:19–20).

- We too will one day have a resurrected body (1 Corinthians 15:42–44).

- We receive that resurrected body when Jesus returns (1 Thessalonians 4:16–17).

Do not fear. Although the body awaits resurrection, when you die your spirit immediately goes to be with the Lord.

Picture it like this:

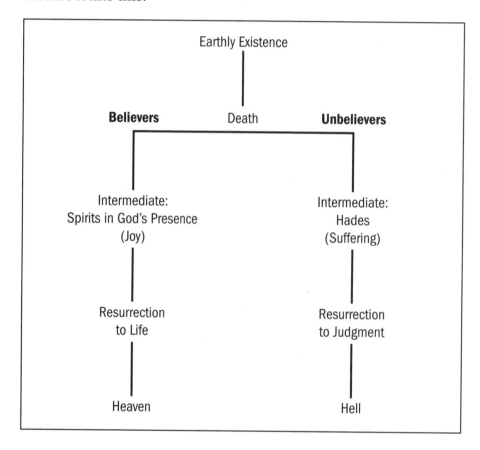

Key Personal Perspective

How Can I Be Sure I Won't Spend Eternity in Hell?

What kind of crime does a person have to commit to be sent to such a horrible place? The crime that will send a person to hell is:

_____ Jesus Christ as the Son of God, the Savior we all need.

> For God so loved the world that he gave his one and only Son, that whoever believes in him shall not perish but have eternal life. For God did not send his Son into the world to condemn the world, but to save the world through him. Whoever believes in him is not condemned, but whoever does not believe stands condemned already because he has not believed in the name of God's one and only Son.
>
> —John 3:16–18

Remember: If you decide (by desire or by neglect) to live separate from God in this life, you'll live separate from him in the next life! But if you accept God's offer of a relationship with him through Jesus in this life, you'll live with God in the next life!

Begin working on memory card 9, "The Truth about the Afterlife."

Discussion Questions

1. What do you think most strongly influences most people's beliefs and opinions about the afterlife?
   - The Bible
   - Other world religions
   - New Age thinking
   - Wishful thinking
   - Movies and television
   - Other _____

2. We've learned that there is a hell. What is it that most clearly reminds you that hell is a real place? Why is it important that there is a hell?

3. Take some time together as a group to pray two things:

   • Prayers of praise for Jesus' willing sacrifice on the cross to save us from hell.

   • Prayers for those you know who have not yet trusted Christ to save them.

4. Why do you think the Bible so clearly and graphically tells us that hell is a place of suffering?

5. How does it make you feel to realize that you, as a Christian, will never have to stand before God to be judged on whether you'll be in heaven or hell—it's already settled! Talk together about the confidence and the joy of knowing that we've already made the most important decision in our lives.

 ## Answers to Fill-Ins

Jesus

Satan and his angels

on earth

lake of fire

don't give up hope

trust them to God

Hades

Abraham's bosom, paradise

no rest

second chances

rejecting

The Afterlife
Part 2

Life Change Objectives

- Joy!!

- To decide to live in the light of eternity in one significant way the next week.

> I strain to reach the end of the race and receive the prize for which God, through Christ Jesus, is calling us up to heaven.
>
> —Philippians 3:14 (NLT)

God has created men and women with a sense that this life is not all there is. The Bible says,

> He has also set eternity in the hearts of men.
>
> —Ecclesiastes 3:11

All of us know instinctively that the grave is not our final destiny. In the last session we explored what the afterlife will be like for unbelievers.

Many questions remain about the specifics of the afterlife for believers:

Where is heaven?

Who will be in heaven?

How will I be judged as a believer?

What will heaven be like?

How can heaven affect my life now?

Where Is Heaven?

Heaven is _____

> LORD, I look up to you, up to heaven, where you rule.
>
> —Psalm 123:1 (GNT)

In the Old Testament, heaven is spoken of figuratively in terms of layers of sky. The heavens are where the birds fly, the trees breathe, and the rain falls. This was referred to as the _____.

The heavens are also where the moon and stars move in their orbits. This was referred to as the _____.

The _____, or highest heaven, was said to be where God dwells in a special way.

Heaven is _____

Heaven is God's _____ and the _____ of believers.

> I heard a loud shout from the throne, saying, "Look, the home of God is now among his people! He will live with them, and they will be his people. God himself will be with them."
>
> —Revelation 21:3 (NLT)

One of the names given to heaven is the _____.

> But they were looking for a better place, a heavenly homeland. That is why God is not ashamed to be called their God, for he has prepared a heavenly city for them.
>
> —Hebrews 11:16 (NLT)

Who Will Be in Heaven?

In Hebrews 12:22–23 we're told of many inhabitants:

> But you have come to Mount Zion, to the city of the living God, the heavenly Jerusalem. You have come to thousands of angels gathered together with joy. You have come to the meeting of God's firstborn children whose names are written in heaven. You have come to God, the judge of all people, and to the spirits of good people who have been made perfect.
>
> —Hebrews 12:22–23 (NCV)

This passage tells us that in heaven there will be:

Angels

God

The church

Old Testament believers

As we saw in the last study, the only people who will spend eternity with God are those who choose him in this life.

> That if you confess with your mouth, "Jesus is Lord," and believe in your heart that God raised him from the dead, you will be saved.
>
> —Romans 10:9

A Closer Look

Will babies or children who die go to heaven? *Yes!* Although they are not old enough to be saved, they are kept safe by God's grace. A child (or someone who is mentally handicapped) who dies before reaching the age that they can understand their sin and need for Christ will not be held accountable for what they cannot understand. That would violate both God's justice and God's grace. Although the Bible does not directly answer this question, we can see two specific indications that the answer is yes.

1. God is just and righteous in everything he does.

   > The LORD is righteous in all his ways and loving toward all he has made.
   >
   > —Psalm 145:17

   He will not make a mistake in any of his judgments.

2. David believed that he would be reunited with his baby who had died (2 Sam. 12:23).

How Will I Be Judged as a Believer?

The Bible tells us of two times of judgment at the end of the world:

1. The _____

   At this judgment those who do not believe in Christ will hear their final judgment and sentencing of separation from God. Those who trust in Christ will not face this judgment.

2. The _____

   In speaking to the believers in Corinth, Paul writes:

   > For we must all appear before the judgment seat of Christ, that each one may receive what is due him for the things done while in the body, whether good or bad.
   >
   > —2 Corinthians 5:10

   Bema is the Greek word translated "judgment seat" in these verses.

The nature of the bema judgment

By the grace God has given me, I laid a foundation as an expert builder, and someone else is building on it. But each one should be careful how he builds. For no one can lay any foundation other than the one already laid, which is Jesus Christ. If any man builds on this foundation using gold, silver, costly stones, wood, hay or straw, his work will be shown for what it is, because the Day will bring it to light. It will be revealed with fire, and the fire will test the quality of each man's work. If what he has built survives, he will receive his reward. If it is burned up, he will suffer loss; he himself will be saved, but only as one escaping through the flames.

—1 Corinthians 3:10–15

1. What we've built into our lives that will last will be _____.

2. What we've built into our lives that will not last will be _____.

3. Whatever our rewards or loss, our salvation is _____.

Therefore judge nothing before the appointed time; wait till the Lord comes. He will bring to light what is hidden in darkness and will expose the motives of men's hearts. At that time each will receive his praise from God.

—1 Corinthians 4:5

A Closer Look

We're told in Scripture that believers will be rewarded based on three specifics:

1. _____

For the Son of Man is going to come in his Father's glory with his angels, and then he will reward each person according to what he has done.

—Matthew 16:27

2. _____

I the LORD search the heart and examine the mind, to reward a man according to his conduct, according to what his deeds deserve.

—Jeremiah 17:10

3. _____

But I tell you that men will have to give account on the day of judgment for every careless word they have spoken.

—Matthew 12:36

What Will Heaven Be Like?

Six truths to bring you joy

You have made known to me the path of life; you will fill me with joy in your presence, with eternal pleasures at your right hand.

—Psalm 16:11

1. Holiness

And now, all glory to God, who is able to keep you from stumbling, and who will bring you into his glorious presence innocent of sin and with great joy.

—Jude 1:24 (NLT)

Dear friends, now we are children of God, and we have not yet been shown what we will be in the future. But we know that when Christ comes again, we will be like him, because we will see him as he really is.

—1 John 3:2 (NCV)

2. A glorified body

Now we know that if the earthly tent we live in is destroyed, we have a building from God, an eternal house in heaven, not built by human hands.

—2 Corinthians 5:1

For while we are in this tent, we groan and are burdened, because we do not wish to be unclothed but to be clothed with our heavenly dwelling, so that what is mortal may be swallowed up by life.

—2 Corinthians 5:4

3. Immortality

He will wipe every tear from their eyes. There will be no more death or mourning or crying or pain, for the old order of things has passed away.

—Revelation 21:4

For our earthly bodies, the ones we have now that can die, must be transformed into heavenly bodies that cannot perish but will live forever.

—1 Corinthians 15:53 (LB)

4. Satisfaction of all needs

Never again will they hunger; never again will they thirst. The sun will not beat upon them, nor any scorching heat.

—Revelation 7:16

5. Sharing of Christ's glory

Now if we are children, then we are heirs—heirs of God and co-heirs with Christ, if indeed we share in his sufferings in order that we may also share in his glory.

—Romans 8:17

6. Intimate fellowship with God and other believers

Now we see but a poor reflection as in a mirror; then we shall see face to face. Now I know in part; then I shall know fully, even as I am fully known.

—1 Corinthians 13:12

How Can Heaven Affect My Life Now?

Let's look at five specific areas that can affect our lives now by being heavenly minded.

1. Motivation for _____

   Jesus answered, "I am the way and the truth and the life. No one comes to the Father except through me."

   —John 14:6

   This is what God told us: God has given us eternal life, and this life is in his Son. Whoever has the Son has life, but whoever does not have the Son of God does not have life.

   —1 John 5:11–12 (NCV)

2. Wise use of _____

   Don't store treasures for yourselves here on earth where moths and rust will destroy them and thieves can break in and steal them. But store your treasures in heaven where they cannot be destroyed by moths or rust and where thieves cannot break in and steal them. Your heart will be where your treasure is.

   —Matthew 6:19–21 (NCV)

3. Serving the _____

   Then the King will say to those on his right, "Come, you who are blessed by my Father; take your inheritance, the kingdom prepared for you since the creation of the world. For I was hungry and you gave me something to eat, I was thirsty and you gave me something to drink, I was a stranger and you invited me in, I needed clothes and you clothed me, I was sick and you looked after me, I was in prison and you came to visit me." Then the righteous will answer him, "Lord, when did we see you hungry and feed you, or thirsty and give you something to drink? When did we see you a stranger and invite you in, or needing clothes and clothe you? When did we see you sick or in prison and go to visit you?" The King will reply, "I tell you the truth, whatever you did for one of the least of these brothers of mine, you did for me."

   —Matthew 25:34–40

Listen, Christian

I was hungry, and you formed a humanities club and discussed my hunger. Thank you.

I was imprisoned and you crept off quietly to your chapel in the cellar and prayed for my release.

I was naked and in your mind you debated the morality of my appearance.

I was sick and you knelt and thanked God for your health.

I was homeless and you preached to me of the spiritual shelter of the love of God.

I was lonely and you left me alone to pray for me.

You seem so holy, so close to God. But I am still very hungry, and lonely, and cold.

Thank you.[1]

4. Endurance in _____

So we do not give up. Our physical body is becoming older and weaker, but our spirit inside us is made new every day. We have small troubles for a while now, but they are helping us gain an eternal glory that is much greater than the troubles. We set our eyes not on what we see but on what we cannot see. What we see will last only a short time, but what we cannot see will last forever.

—2 Corinthians 4:16–18 (NCV)

5. Easing of _____

Since you became alive again, so to speak, when Christ arose from the dead, now set your sights on the rich treasures and joys of heaven where he sits beside God in the place of honor and power. Let heaven fill your thoughts; don't spend your time worrying about things down here.

—Colossians 3:1–2 (LB)

Acting on the Truth

God's Word repeatedly instructs us to shift our focus from earthly matters to focus on God's perspective. Take seven minutes at the beginning or the end of the day for a week to focus on these seven truths:

1. His plan for me will never change.

2. My salvation is safe and secure in heaven, where nothing can destroy it.

3. When he comes for me I will go with him to the home he carefully and lovingly has been preparing for me.

4. Nothing can ever separate me from his love—no pain, no suffering, no tragedy, no hardship, no demon, no horrible mistake on my part, nothing!

5. I am to spend my days learning to love him and to trust him.

6. I am to be his arms and hands of compassion to fellow human beings.

7. And someday, I will join millions of other believers at his throne, and together we will worship him. We will sing with the angels,

Worthy is the Lamb, who was slain, to receive power and wealth and wisdom and strength and honor and glory and praise!

—Revelation 5:12

Finish memorizing memory card 9, "The Truth about the Afterlife."

Discussion Questions

1. Do some brainstorming together for a few moments about how great heaven will be by giving one-line completions to the following statements. Have fun with this!

   The greatest thing about heaven will be that I won't have to . . .

   The greatest thing about heaven will be that I will be able to . . .

   A picture that helps me to think of the greatness of heaven is . . .

   In heaven there will be an abundant supply of . . .

   In heaven there will be no . . .

   Someone I'm looking forward to meeting in heaven is . . .

   Something I'm looking forward to doing in heaven is . . .

2. First Corinthians 3:10–15 says that believers who build the wrong things into their lives will "suffer loss" but will be saved. What do you think are some of the things that we build into our lives now that will be "burned up"? What are some of the things that will last? What kind of loss do you think we will suffer?

3. Look again at the list of six things that describe "what heaven will be like." Which two sound the most attractive to you right now? Which one is difficult to understand?

4. How would you like your glorified body to look? What would you like it to be able to do?

5. In what way would you like the truth of heaven to have a greater impact on your daily life?

For Further Study

Elwell, Walter, ed. *Topical Analysis of the Bible*. Grand Rapids, Mich.: Baker, 1991.

Evans, Louis H., Sr. *Your Thrilling Future*. Wheaton, Ill.: Tyndale, 1982.

Gilmore, John. *Probing Heaven*. Grand Rapids, Mich.: Baker, 1989.

Habermas, Gary R. *Immortality: The Other Side of Death*. Nashville: Nelson, 1992.

Hybels, Bill. "Your Everafter: Heaven." Audiotape. Carol Stream, Ill.: Preaching Today, n.d.

Morey, Dr. Robert A. *Death and the Afterlife*. Minneapolis: Bethany, 1984.

Rhodes, Ron. *Heaven: The Undiscovered Country*. Eugene, Ore.: Harvest House, 1995.

Toon, Peter. *Heaven and Hell*. Nashville: Nelson, 1986.

Answers to Fill-Ins

up   lost
first heaven   secure
second heaven   actions
third heaven   thoughts
home   words
dwelling place   evangelism
final dwelling place   finances
heavenly city   needy
Great White Throne judgment   suffering
"bema" judgment   anxieties
rewarded

The Church
Part 1

Life Change Objectives
• To deepen your love for and commitment to the church.
• To see in a new or deeper way your part in living out all five purposes of the church.

As we begin this study of the church of God, some may ask, "Why is the church so important? Why can't I just have a relationship with Jesus and forget about the church?" We all know people who consider themselves Christians but seldom attend church. Is the church really necessary?

Absolutely! To have faith in God means we cannot live the Christian life in isolation, like a spiritual Robinson Crusoe. The truth is, we cannot live out the Christian life without belonging to the church. The New Testament knows nothing of unattached Christians.

Our Need for the Church

God's Ideal	Our Actual Practice
Church is a spiritual necessity	Church is an optional activity
Interdependence is valued	Individualism is valued
Spirituality takes place in community	Religion is a private matter
Active involvement in social concerns	Aloof from the real world
All people fully accepted together	Segregation practiced (racial, social status, etc.)
Authentic behavior, with the public and private lives matching	Hypocrisy; saying one thing but practicing another

To recapture the role God intended for us as his church, we must gain an understanding of how the church began, what its nature is, what its mission is, and explore the implications for *our* church.

The Beginning of the Church

_____ *by God*

The Bible makes it clear that God has always desired to create a people for himself; a people who would love him with all their hearts, and a people for whom he could prove himself to be a faithful God.

> For you are a people holy to the LORD your God. The LORD your God has chosen you out of all the peoples on the face of the earth to be his people, his treasured possession.
>
> —Deuteronomy 7:6

A Closer Look

When Adam turned away from the blessing of being in harmony with God, God turned to creating a people for himself. He called Abraham, Isaac, and Jacob to be the forefathers of these people—Israel. When Israel proved to be unfaithful to God's covenant promises, God continued his plan through a "remnant" of people, who also became unfaithful to him. God's plan came to fruition when he sent his Son, Jesus, to bring together finally a people who would belong totally to God. These people would be an "elect race, a royal priesthood, a holy nation, a people of God's possession." This is the church.

> But you are a chosen people, a royal priesthood, a holy nation, a people belonging to God, that you may declare the praises of him who called you out of darkness into his wonderful light.
>
> —1 Peter 2:9

_____ *by Jesus*

In Matthew 16:18, Jesus says, "I will build my church, and the gates of hell will not prevail against it." This indicates that the church was still in the future when he spoke. He was making a prediction concerning his future building of the church.

_____ *by the Spirit*

How is the church built? It is the work of the Holy Spirit baptizing believers into the body of Christ.

> For we were all baptized by one Spirit into one body—whether Jews or Greeks, slave or free—and we were all given the one Spirit to drink.
>
> —1 Corinthians 12:13

The Nature of the Church
(What is it supposed to be?)

The church is an _____.

The primary Greek word used for the church in the New Testament is *ekklesia,* which has the meaning "to call." It was used to describe an assembly of people (secular or spiritual), but it came to mean an assembly or community called by God. So the assembling was not the key. The key was the fact that God called them together.

Ekklesia refers to both the _____ church and the _____ church.

The universal church is composed of people from every tribe and race and culture (regardless of their denominational affiliations) who have accepted Jesus Christ as their Lord and Savior.

In the universal church the emphasis is on the _____ of the church.

The local church is a group of believers who meet together for worship, instruction, fellowship, and ministry.

In the local church, the emphasis is on the _____ of the church.

The church is a _____.

Another important Greek word that relates to the church is *koinonia.* Difficult to translate into English, it carries the idea of communion, fellowship, sharing, and participation. It is used to describe the life that the *ekklesia,* or church, is to share in Christ.

Koinonia is our participation together in the life of God through Jesus Christ.

Koinonia is:

- more than the congenial relationship of "buddies."
- more than participating in a potluck dinner.
- more than "I can get along with you because you're so much like me."

Koinonia is a oneness that is possible only through God's supernatural work.

Koinonia is characterized by:

- _____ (1 John 1:6–7)
- _____ (Phil. 2:1–2)
- _____ (Philem. 1:17)

- _____ (Acts 2:44–45)
- _____ (2 Cor. 8:4)
- _____ (Phil. 3:8–10)
- _____ (1 Cor. 10:16)

 ## A Closer Look

The Ordinances of the Church

The word *ordinance* comes from the word *ordained*. It refers to the events that Jesus specifically ordered us to make a regular part of our worship as a church. The two ordinances that Jesus gave to the church are baptism and the Lord's Supper.

Baptism demonstrates _____ what took place _____ when we accepted Christ. Through baptism, our participation in his death, burial, and resurrection is portrayed, and we rise up out of the water, symbolizing the new life we now have in Christ.

Why is it important for you to be baptized as a believer in Christ? First and foremost, because Jesus commanded it! He "ordained" —he commanded—baptism to be a step we take as we follow him. In his Great Commission in Matthew 28:19 and 20, Jesus told us to "Make disciples of all nations, baptizing them in the name of the Father and of the Son and of the Holy Spirit."

When you are baptized, you are picturing to the world what happened in your life when you became a believer. Look at Romans 6:4:

> We were therefore buried with him through baptism into death in order that, just as Christ was raised from the dead through the glory of the Father, we too may live a new life.
>
> —Romans 6:4

The Lord's Supper, or Communion, also is a physical reminder of deep, spiritual realities. We remember that through his broken body and spilled blood a _____ has been established between God and man.

> And when he had given thanks, he broke it and said, "This is my body, which is for you; do this in remembrance of me." In the same way, after supper he took the cup, saying, "This cup is the new covenant in my blood; do this, whenever you drink it, in remembrance of me." For whenever you eat this bread and drink this cup, you proclaim the Lord's death until he comes.
>
> —1 Corinthians 11:24–26

Sometimes the ordinances are called "sacraments," from the Latin *Sacramentum,* which was an oath of allegiance a Roman soldier took to his emperor. Christians took over the term and meant that it bound them in loyalty to Christ. In the ordinances, Christ's grace and forgiveness are depicted—they are sermons acted out. We are allowed the opportunity to express our allegiance and loyalty to Christ when we are baptized and when we eat the Lord's Supper together. The ordinances do not give us "more" of God's grace. They are a way to praise God for the grace we've already received.

The Mission of the Church (What is the church supposed to do?)

The five purposes of the church

The five purposes of the church are given in two statements of Jesus: the Great Commandment and the Great Commission.

The Great Commandment

Jesus replied: "'Love the Lord your God with all your heart and with all your soul and with all your mind.' This is the first and greatest commandment. And the second is like it: 'Love your neighbor as yourself.' All the Law and the Prophets hang on these two commandments."

—Matthew 22:37–40

The Great Commission

Therefore go and make disciples of all nations, baptizing them in the name of the Father and of the Son and of the Holy Spirit, and teaching them to obey everything I have commanded you. And surely I am with you always, to the very end of the age.

—Matthew 28:19–20

Five instructions for the church

1. "Love God with all your heart": _____

2. "Love your neighbor as yourself": _____

3. "Go . . . make disciples": _____

4. "Baptizing them": _____

5. "Teaching them to do": _____

The church exists to:

1. Celebrate God's _____ (worship)

   "Exalt our Master."

   > O magnify the LORD with me, and let us exalt his name together!
   > —Psalm 34:3 (RSV)

   > I was glad when they said to me, "Let us go to the LORD's house."
   > —Psalm 122:1 (GNT)

2. Communicate God's _____ (evangelism)

   "Evangelize our mission field."

   > The most important thing is that I complete my mission, the work that the Lord Jesus gave me—to tell people the Good News about God's grace.
   > —Acts 20:24 (NCV)

   > You will be my witnesses . . .
   > —Acts 1:8

3. Incorporate God's _____ (fellowship)

   "Encourage our members."

   > You are members of God's very own family . . . and you belong in God's household with every other Christian.
   > —Ephesians 2:19 (LB)

4. Educate God's _____ (discipleship)

   "Educate for maturity."

   > Building up the church, the body of Christ, to a position of strength and maturity; until . . . all become full-grown in the Lord.
   > —Ephesians 4:12–13 (LB)

5. Demonstrate God's _____ (ministry)

   "Equip for ministry."

   > To equip the saints for the work of ministry.
   > —Ephesians 4:12 (NRSV)

Purpose Statement for the Church

To bring people to Jesus and to membership in his family, to develop them to Christlike maturity, and to equip them for their ministry in the church and their life mission in the world in order to magnify God's name.

Begin working on memory card 10, "The Truth about the Church."

Discussion Questions

1. How does the idea of the unity of the church really work in your life? Here are some points of struggle that it would be helpful to discuss honestly.

   - How do you handle it when you disagree strongly on some issue (political, for instance) with a Christian brother or sister?

   - How do you survive the temptation to compare: to think "I wish I had their gift" or "I have better gifts than they do. Why are they being noticed more than I am?"

   - Is our unity in Christ always stronger than the prejudices we grew up with? How can that unity break down those prejudices?

2. Look back at the seven characteristics of *koinonia* fellowship. Which of these is the most important to you personally?

3. Suppose you came home to find five phone messages for you from different people:

   - From someone asking you for your opinion about a new mission project.

   - From a friend asking about how to help two fellow Christians with a disagreement they've been having.

   - From someone asking a question about understanding a Bible verse or Bible truth.

   - From another with an idea for starting a new ministry.

   - From a friend who has some questions about how to truly worship God.

All things being equal, which of these calls would you return first?

Answers to Fill-Ins

envisioned	Lord's Supper
established	physically
energized	spiritually
ekklesia	new covenant
universal	worship
local	ministry
unity	evangelism
ministry	fellowship
koinonia	discipleship
light	presence
unity	Word
acceptance	family
sharing of material goods	people
giving money	love
suffering	

The Church
Part 2

Life Change Objectives

- To gain a new appreciation for what the church can be in your life and in the world.

- To let go of false pictures of a perfect church and commit to the true picture of a powerful church (filled with weak people!).

A quick review of the last session:

- The church was envisioned by God.
- The church was established by Jesus.
- The church is energized by the Spirit.

The church was made possible by Jesus' death and resurrection.

Our mandate from God is to live out the Great Commission and the Great Commandment through the five purposes of evangelism, fellowship, discipleship, ministry, and worship.

The New Testament lists sixty-seven names and metaphors for the church, each one giving another dimension and aspect of the nature and mission of the church. Today we'll be looking at five of the most significant metaphors for the church.

The Metaphors for the Church

The body of Christ

The church is Jesus' body and Jesus is the head of the body.

> And God placed all things under his feet and appointed him to be head over everything for the church, which is his body, the fullness of him who fills everything in every way.
>
> —Ephesians 1:22–23

Two words are crucial as we study the body of Christ, the church:

    1. _____   2. _____

Our unity is built upon:

• Christ breaking down the wall of _____.

> For Christ himself is our way of peace. He has made peace between us Jews and you Gentiles by making us all one family, breaking down the wall of contempt that used to separate us.
>
> —Ephesians 2:14 (LB)

• Our _____ in Christ's body.

> By his death he ended the angry resentment between us, caused by the Jewish laws which favored the Jews and excluded the Gentiles, for he died to annul that whole system of Jewish laws. Then he took the two groups that had been opposed to each other and made them parts of himself; thus he fused us together to become one new person, and at last there was peace.
>
> —Ephesians 2:15 (LB)

• Our _____ at the cross.

> As parts of the same body, our anger against each other has disappeared, for both of us have been reconciled to God. And so the feud ended at last at the cross.
>
> —Ephesians 2:16 (LB)

• Our common _____, common _____, and common _____ destination.

> Now you are no longer strangers to God and foreigners to heaven, but you are members of God's very own family, citizens of God's country, and you belong in God's household with every other Christian.
>
> —Ephesians 2:19 (LB)

Key Personal Perspective

How Do I Handle a Disagreement with a Fellow Believer?

The wrong way: _____

> Gossip separates the best of friends.
>
> —Proverbs 16:28 (NLT)

The right way: _____

> If another believer sins against you, go privately and point out the fault. If the other person listens and confesses it, you have won that person back. But if you are unsuccessful, take one or two others with you and go back again, so that everything you say may be confirmed by two or three witnesses. If that person still refuses to listen, take your case to the church. If the church decides you are right, but the other person won't accept it, treat that person as a pagan or a corrupt tax collector.
>
> —Matthew 18:15–17 (NLT)

> Therefore, if you are offering your gift at the altar and there remember that your brother has something against you, leave your gift there in front of the altar. First go and be reconciled to your brother; then come and offer your gift.
>
> —Matthew 5:23–24

Our diversity

> Now the body is not made up of one part but of many. If the foot should say, "Because I am not a hand, I do not belong to the body," it would not for that reason cease to be part of the body. And if the ear should say, "Because I am not an eye, I do not belong to the body," it would not for that reason cease to be part of the body. If the whole body were an eye, where would the sense of hearing be? If the whole body were an ear, where would the sense of smell be?
>
> —1 Corinthians 12:14–17

> Just as each of us has one body with many members, and these members do not all have the same function, so in Christ we who are many form one body, and each member belongs to all the others.
>
> —Romans 12:4–5

The flock of God

> I have other sheep that are not of this sheep pen. I must bring them also. They too will listen to my voice, and there shall be one flock and one shepherd.
>
> —John 10:16

1. We are the sheep.

   This image emphasizes that members of the church, as the sheep of Christ, _____.

   > But you do not believe because you are not my sheep. My sheep listen to my voice; I know them, and they follow me. I give them eternal life, and they shall never perish; no one can snatch them out of my hand. My Father, who has given them to me, is greater than all; no one can snatch them out of my Father's hand.
   >
   > —John 10:26–29

2. Jesus is the shepherd.

   The metaphor of Jesus as our shepherd shows his love and care for us.

   > I am the good shepherd. The good shepherd lays down his life for the sheep. I am the good shepherd; I know my sheep and my sheep know me—just as the Father knows me and I know the Father—and I lay down my life for the sheep. I have other sheep that are not of this sheep pen. I must bring them also. They too will listen to my voice, and there shall be one flock and one shepherd.
   >
   > —John 10:11, 14–16

The family (household) of God

1. God adopts us into his family.

   In the physical world, individuals automatically become part of a family unit when they are born. God wisely made the same provision for his spiritual children as well. At salvation, we are placed by the Holy Spirit into God's family, and God is now our Father.

   > For we were all baptized by one Spirit into one body—whether Jews or Greeks, slave or free—and we were all given the one Spirit to drink.
   >
   > —1 Corinthians 12:13

   > And so we should not be like cringing, fearful slaves, but we should behave like God's very own children, adopted into the bosom of his family, and calling to him, "Father, Father."
   >
   > —Romans 8:15 (LB)

2. We're to treat one another as family.

   > Do not rebuke an older man harshly, but exhort him as if he were your father. Treat younger men as brothers, older women as mothers, and younger women as sisters, with absolute purity.
   >
   > —1 Timothy 5:1–2

The building of God

You are also God's building (1 Cor. 3:9 TEV).

In contrast to the Old Testament period in which Israel _____ a temple (Ex. 25:8), the church _____ a temple: a living, vital temple.

> Consequently, you are no longer foreigners and aliens, but fellow citizens with God's people and members of God's household, built on the foundation of the apostles and prophets, with Christ Jesus himself as the chief cornerstone. In him the whole building is joined together and rises to become a holy temple in the Lord. And in him you too are being built together to become a dwelling in which God lives by his Spirit.
> —Ephesians 2:19–22

In this metaphor, Jesus is pictured as the _____.

The cornerstone was placed at the juncture of two walls to tie them together. In arches, a stone was placed between the supporting sides. The weight of the arch was on that stone, and if the stone was removed, the arch could collapse.

Individual believers are pictured as _____.

In the construction of the church as a temple, each stone is a living stone because it shares the divine nature, and the building as a whole becomes a dwelling place for God through his Spirit.

> As you come to him, the living Stone—rejected by men but chosen by God and precious to him—you also, like living stones, are being built into a spiritual house to be a holy priesthood, offering spiritual sacrifices acceptable to God through Jesus Christ.
> —1 Peter 2:4–5

Key Personal Perspective

How readily do you accept believers from other denominations and churches as being "real" Christians? Have you been trying to carry all the weight of the Christian life on your shoulders? Do you need to see the importance of your place in God's building? Do you need to recognize your need to depend on others in the body of Christ?

The bride of Christ

This is the one metaphor that is used of the church in a prophetic sense.

- Israel was often portrayed in the Old Testament as being the _____ or _____ of God.

    And I will make you my promised bride forever. I will be good and fair; I will show you my love and mercy. I will be true to you as my promised bride, and you will know the LORD.

    —Hosea 2:19–20 (NCV)

- However, Israel was repeatedly _____ to her vows of love to God.

    This message from the Lord came to me during the reign of King Josiah: Have you seen what Israel does? Like a wanton wife who gives herself to other men at every chance, so Israel has worshiped other gods on every hill, beneath every shady tree. I thought that someday she would return to me and once again be mine; but she didn't come back. And her faithless sister Judah saw the continued rebellion of Israel.

    —Jeremiah 3:6–7 (LB)

- Unlike faithless Israel, the church is portrayed in Scripture as being a _____ awaiting the coming of her bridegroom.

    I am jealous for you with a godly jealousy. I promised you to one husband, to Christ, so that I might present you as a pure virgin to him.

    —2 Corinthians 11:2

In Ephesians 5:22–33, the analogy is drawn comparing the husband and wife relationship in marriage to Christ and his bride, the church. The illustration is powerful because it reveals the magnitude of Christ's love for his church. He loved her enough to die for her. It also reveals the obedient response the church is to have to the bridegroom, Jesus Christ.

> Husbands, love your wives, just as Christ loved the church and gave himself up for her to make her holy, cleansing her by the washing with water through the word.
>
> —Ephesians 5:25–26

- The relationship of the bride to the Bridegroom reflects two characteristics of the nature of the church:

    1. The church lives with a sense of urgency to always be _____ for the Bridegroom.

        At that time the kingdom of heaven will be like ten virgins who took their lamps and went out to meet the bridegroom. Five of them were foolish and five were wise. The foolish ones took their lamps but did not take any oil with them. The wise, however, took oil in jars along with their lamps. The bridegroom was a long time in coming, and they all became drowsy and fell asleep. At midnight the cry rang out: "Here's the bridegroom! Come out to meet him!" Then all the virgins woke up and trimmed their lamps. The foolish ones said to the wise, "Give us some of your oil; our lamps are going out." "No," they replied, "there may not be enough for both us and you. Instead, go to those who sell oil and buy some for yourselves." But while they were on their way to buy the oil, the bridegroom arrived. The virgins who were ready went in with him to the wedding banquet. And the door was shut. Later the others also came. "Sir! Sir!" they said. "Open the door for us!" But he replied, "I tell you the truth, I don't know you." Therefore keep watch, because you do not know the day or the hour.

—Matthew 25:1–13

2. The church is to _____ into the new relationship with the Bridegroom.

Then he said to his servants, "The wedding banquet is ready, but those I invited did not deserve to come. Go to the street corners and invite to the banquet anyone you find."

—Matthew 22:8–9

Blessed are those who are invited to the wedding supper of the Lamb!

—Revelation 19:9

The Spirit and the bride say, "Come!" And let him who hears say, "Come!" Whoever is thirsty, let him come; and whoever wishes, let him take the free gift of the water of life.

—Revelation 22:17

Key Personal Perspective

Being the bride of Christ is a spiritual love affair. Is this a reality in your life? Or does the idea seem too sentimental? Is there submission in your heart to Jesus as your Bridegroom? Are you ready to meet him? Are there some priorities you need to rearrange so that you can concentrate more on loving him?

A Final Word

Is the church of God a useless, worn-out institution? It doesn't have to be. God has made all the provisions necessary for local churches to be vibrant, transformational groups of believers who live interdependent, authentic lives of ministry and mission, building bridges so that lost people can find hope in God. The Devil can't stop us; the pervasive culture around us can't stop us. We are the only ones who can cause the church to lose its place of importance by not acting like the body of Christ, the flock of God, the family of God, the building of God, and the bride of Christ.

> I will build my church, and the gates of Hades will not overcome it!
> —Matthew 16:18

> **Finish memorizing memory card 10,**
> **"The Truth about the Church," before the next session.**
> **We're sure there will be a quiz on these cards**
> **when you get to heaven!**

Discussion Questions

In our group discussion, we're going to look back at the questions we've asked about how the pictures of the church challenge us in a *personal* way.

1. *The church is the body of Christ:* every part of the body is important. (What part would *you* want to give up?) Do you feel like you're an important part of the body of Christ?

2. *The church is the flock of God:* what are the things that we can do that make sure that Jesus is the shepherd leading us, that we aren't trying to lead ourselves?

3. *The church is the family of God:* how does this help you to picture your responsibilities toward other believers?

4. *The church is the building of God:* how readily do you accept believers from other denominations and churches as being "real" Christians? Have you been trying to carry all of the weight of the Christian life on your shoulders? Do you need to see the importance of your place in God's building? Do you need to recognize your need to depend on others in the body of Christ?

5. *The church is the bride of Christ:* being the bride of Christ is a spiritual love affair. Is this a reality in your life? Or does the idea seem too sentimental? Is there submission in your heart to Jesus as your Bridegroom? Is your life ready to meet him? Are there some priorities you need to rearrange so that you can concentrate more on loving him?

For Further Study

Getz, Gene. *Sharpening the Focus of the Church.* Chicago: Moody Press, 1974.

MacArthur, John, Jr. *Body Dynamics.* Wheaton, Ill.: Victor, 1983.

Moore, John, and Ken Neff. *A New Testament Blueprint for the Church.* Chicago: Moody Press, 1985.

Radmacher, Earl D. *The Nature of the Church.* Portland, Ore.: Western Baptist Press, 1972.

Warren, Rick. *The Purpose-Driven Church.* Grand Rapids, Mich.: Zondervan, 1995.

Answers to Fill-Ins

unity	belong to him
diversity	had
separation	is
oneness	chief cornerstone
equal standing	living stones
citizenship	wife, bride
family	unfaithful
future	virgin bride
gossip	prepared
confront it	invite others

The Second Coming
Part 1

Life Change Objective

That you will see the Second Coming not as a source of confusion or fear but as a source of hope.

What do you feel about the truth of Jesus' Second Coming?

Apathy? Anticipation? Anxiety?

Any study of the Second Coming has to come with some "warning labels" attached.

Warning: **Don't lose personal _____ in the midst of historical and theological _____.**

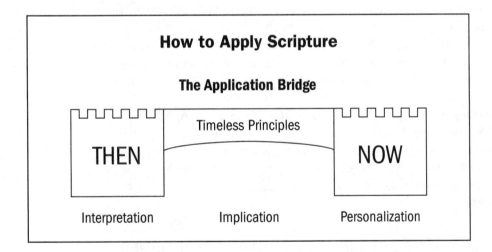

How to Apply Scripture

The Application Bridge

Timeless Principles

THEN — NOW

Interpretation — Implication — Personalization

1. What did the Bible passage mean to the original hearers?

   Much of the prophecy about the Second Coming is apocalyptic literature (from the Greek word *apocalypse*, "to unveil, to reveal"), a type of writing designed to make the truth clear to some while hiding it from others.

2. What is the underlying timeless principle?

In a word, _____.

The Scriptures concerning Jesus' Second Coming not only talk about hope for the believers living at that time but about hope for us. It's obvious as you read that we're looking at many prophecies that have yet to be fulfilled.

3. Where or how could I practice this principle?

As much as we talk about the time and events of the Second Coming, the Bible emphasizes the application of this truth in our lives. *It is a sin* to study the Second Coming looking only for timetables. The message of hope must make an impact on the way we live.

Remember:

It is a message to obey, not just to listen to (James 1:22).

Knowing what is right to do and then not doing it is sin (James 4:17).

Far too many believers have a fascination with the future without any application for today.

Warning: **Don't lose the _____ in the _____.**

> Once in the Louvre Museum in Paris, I stood inches away from a large impressionistic painting by Renoir. "What in the world is that?" I wondered aloud. My wife answered, "Stand back, Bill, and you will see it." I had stepped too close to the masterpiece and each individual detail, each oil splotch of color, each brush stroke kept me from seeing the whole. I was bogged down by the details. But when I stood back, the mysterious puzzle disappeared and the beautiful vision of the artist formed in my brain.
>
> For too long, too many of us have stood too close to the Apocalypse of John. We have turned that great masterpiece into a series of blotches and brush marks. We have tried to outguess each other at the modern meaning of every star, every dragon, and every number, and we have lost the grand design of the prophet's vision and have missed the urgency of his warnings.[1]
>
> —Billy Graham

Warning: **Watch out for "polarization" in teaching about the Second Coming.**

When it comes to teaching about the Second Coming, it's good to spend some time at the "equator" before being drawn away by the magnetic attraction of the "polar regions." In other words, look at the whole truth before being drawn aside by one or another slant on the truth.

In the next two sessions we'll be looking together at:
- The signs of the return of Jesus
- The time of the Second Coming
- The "cast of characters" involved in Jesus' return
- The events surrounding the return of Jesus
- The meaning for my everyday life

 A Closer Look

Is the Second Coming of Christ an important perspective that God wants us to have?

Just remember . . .

One out of every 30 verses in the Bible mentions the subject of the end of time, or of Christ's return.

There are 216 chapters in the New Testament. There are well over 300 references to the return of Christ in the New Testament.

Only four of the 27 New Testament books fail to mention Christ's return.[2]

—Chuck Swindoll

Signs of Jesus' Coming

Three types of signs:
1. Signs pointing to the end (the beginning of birth pains)
2. Signs immediately preceding the end time events
3. Signs accompanying the end time events

Signs pointing to the end

There are a number of things that Jesus said would happen before his Second Coming. He called these the "beginning of birth pains." These are signs, but not signs that we will see only at the very end. They are signs that have shown believers for 2,000 years that this world is not God's final plan. These are signs that we can see now. They are the signs of the deterioration and inadequacy of this world. For thousands of years we've been able to look at these and say, "This world is not as stable as it sometimes seems. Jesus could be coming at any moment!"

Jesus said to them: "Watch out that no one deceives you. Many will come in my name, claiming 'I am he,' and will deceive many. When you hear of wars and rumors of wars, do not be alarmed. Such things must happen, but the end is still to come. Nation will rise against nation, and kingdom against kingdom. There will be earthquakes in various places, and famines. These are the beginning of birth pains."

—Mark 13:5–8

- _____ (with false signs and miracles)

- Wars

- Earthquakes

- Famine

These signs that point to the end will all be summed up at the end. There will be wars, leading to a great final war. There will be false christs with false signs, leading to a great final Antichrist with great false signs that fool many (2 Thess. 2:9; Rev. 19:20). There will be famine in various places, leading to a great worldwide famine in the end (Rev. 6:5–6).

There are indications for the wise to see throughout history. And there are signs that no one could miss at the end of time. It's the difference between hearing a grinding noise under the hood of your car and seeing the engine fall out!

Jesus' warning about these signs: _____!

Signs preceding the end

- _____

At that time many will turn away from the faith and will betray and hate each other.

—Matthew 24:10

For the time will come when men will not put up with sound doctrine. Instead, to suit their own desires, they will gather around them a great number of teachers to say what their itching ears want to hear.

—2 Timothy 4:3

- _____ of personal evil

But mark this: There will be terrible times in the last days. People will be lovers of themselves, lovers of money, boastful, proud, abusive, disobedient to their parents, ungrateful, unholy, without love, unforgiving, slanderous, without self-control, brutal, not lovers of the good, treacherous, rash, conceited, lovers of pleasure rather than lovers of God—having a form of godliness but denying its power. Have nothing to do with them.

—2 Timothy 3:1–5

Brother will betray brother to death, and a father his child. Children will rebel against their parents and have them put to death.

—Mark 13:12

* _____ will come

First of all, you must understand that in the last days scoffers will come, scoffing and following their own evil desires.

—2 Peter 3:3

* Many false prophets

And many false prophets will appear and deceive many people.

—Matthew 24:11

Signs accompanying the end

* Signs in the sun, moon, and stars

There will be signs in the sun, moon and stars.

—Luke 21:25

Immediately after the distress of those days "the sun will be darkened, and the moon will not give its light; the stars will fall from the sky, and the heavenly bodies will be shaken."

—Matthew 24:29

* Roaring of the sea, heavenly bodies shaken

On the earth, nations will be in anguish and perplexity at the roaring and tossing of the sea.

—Luke 21:25

Men will faint from terror, apprehensive of what is coming on the world, for the heavenly bodies will be shaken. At that time they will see the Son of Man coming in a cloud with power and great glory.

—Luke 21:26–27

* Great distress (unparalleled)

For then there will be great distress, unequaled from the beginning of the world until now—and never to be equaled again.

—Matthew 24:21

A Closer Look

The most detailed descriptions of the end time events are found in the book of Revelation.

The seven seals (Final Conflict)	The seven trumpets (Final Destruction)	The seven bowls (God's Wrath Is Finished)
1. White horse: Conquest	1. Earth	1. Sores
2. Red horse: War	2. Sea	2. Sea to blood
3. Black Horse: Famine	3. Rivers	3. Rivers to blood
4. Pale Horse: Death	4. Lights (3 woes)	4. Fire from sun
5. Martyrs	5. Demons (Locusts) into darkness	5. Beast's kingdom
6. Earthquakes	6. Angels and earthquakes (1/3 of men)	6. Euphrates River dried up (Armageddon)
7. The 7th seal is the 7 trumpets	7. The 7th trumpet is the 7 bowls	7. Earthquake (It is done!)

Don't think of John's vivid language as a barrier to understanding; see it instead as the way he painted the picture of God's plan for the future in incredibly vivid colors.[3]

—Billy Graham

In an earlier study we looked at what happens to people after they die. The Bible also very clearly explains to us exactly how this world will end. And it is heading to an inevitable end.

The heavens will disappear with a roar; the elements will be destroyed by fire, and the earth and everything in it will be laid bare. . . . That day will bring about the destruction of the heavens by fire, and the elements will melt in the heat.

—2 Peter 3:10, 12

That's not the end of the story!

Then I saw a new heaven and a new earth, for the first heaven and the first earth had passed away.

—Revelation 21:1

The Time of the Second Coming

Descriptions by Jesus

• Like a _____ (Matt. 25:1–13)

• Like the destruction of Sodom

It was the same in the days of Lot. People were eating and drinking, buying and selling, planting and building. But the day Lot left Sodom, fire and sulfur rained down from heaven and destroyed them all. It will be just like this on the day the Son of Man is revealed.

—Luke 17:28–30

• Like _____

When the Son of Man comes again, it will be as it was when Noah lived. People were eating, drinking, marrying, and giving their children to be married until the day Noah entered the boat. Then the flood came and killed them all.

—Luke 17:26–27 (NCV)

• Like a _____ in the _____

Therefore keep watch, because you do not know on what day your Lord will come. But understand this: If the owner of the house had known at what time of night the thief was coming, he would have kept watch and would not have let his house be broken into. So you also must be ready, because the Son of Man will come at an hour when you do not expect him.

—Matthew 24:42–44

Facts about the timing

• The time of Jesus' return is _____.

Behold, I am coming soon! Blessed is he who keeps the words of the prophecy in this book.

—Revelation 22:7

• The time of Jesus' return is known only by God.

No one knows about that day or hour, not even the angels in heaven, nor the Son, but only the Father.

—Matthew 24:36

So when they met together, they asked him, "Lord, are you at this time going to restore the kingdom to Israel?" He said to them: "It is not for you to know the times or dates the Father has set by his own authority."

—Acts 1:6–7

• The time of Jesus' return is _____.

For you know very well that the day of the Lord will come like a thief in the night.

—1 Thessalonians 5:2

So you also must be ready, because the Son of Man will come at an hour when you do not expect him.

—Matthew 24:44

People of the End Times

1. The Man of Lawlessness/The Beast/The Antichrist

> Don't let anyone deceive you in any way, for that day will not come until the rebellion occurs and the man of lawlessness is revealed, the man doomed to destruction.
>
> —2 Thessalonians 2:3

Hollywood is fascinated by this "ultimate villain." In their zeal they often miss the simple truths Paul tells us in 2 Thessalonians:

> He will oppose and will exalt himself over everything that is called God or is worshiped, so that he sets himself up in God's temple, proclaiming himself to be God. . . . The coming of the lawless one will be in accordance with the work of Satan displayed in all kinds of counterfeit miracles, signs and wonders, and in every sort of evil that deceives those who are perishing.
>
> —2 Thessalonians 2:4, 9–10

 ### A Closer Look

This will be one final Antichrist among many—the end of a long line that began after Jesus' first coming. The Beast is the final and worst Antichrist, not the *only* Antichrist.

> For many will come in my name, claiming, "I am the Christ," and will deceive many.
>
> —Matthew 24:5

> Dear children, this is the last hour; and as you have heard that the antichrist is coming, even now many antichrists have come. This is how we know it is the last hour. . . . Who is the liar? It is the man who denies that Jesus is the Christ. Such a man is the antichrist—he denies the Father and the Son.
>
> —1 John 2:18, 22

There are a number of biblical pictures attached to the Antichrist. These pictures are the subject of literally thousands of prophetic speculations!

- The woman/Babylon—riding the Beast
- 7 heads
- 7 hills on which the woman sits
- 7 kings—5 have fallen, one is, the other is yet to come
- In Revelation 17 the Beast is identified as "an eighth king"
- 666—the number of the Beast
- The 10 horns = 10 kings who will serve along with the Beast

A Closer Look

Revelation is an example of the double application of prophecy, both to those to whom it was originally written and to the saints at a later time.

Jesus' first coming had many examples of this double application of prophecy. Prophecies that were fulfilled in a partial way in Old Testament events found their ultimate and complete fulfillment in the life of Christ.

The book of Revelation obviously points to the Roman Empire and the emperor Domitian in its pictures of the Beast. But it is also just as obvious that there is a greater fulfillment to be seen here—one that can come only at the end of time.

Is it wrong to speculate about what these pictures might mean? No, as long as you never confuse speculation about God's Word with the perfect truth of God's Word. During World War II many believers were absolutely certain that Hitler was the Antichrist. They turned out to be wrong. We must have the humility to recognize that we could be just as wrong about many of our speculations today.

2. A second beast/the _____

   In order to promote his program more efficiently, the Antichrist will have an important lieutenant. He is the "second beast" (Rev. 13:11–18), and his sole duty is to promote the purposes and expedite the worship of the first Beast, the Man of Sin.

3. The two _____

   Revelation 11 talks about two witnesses who will prophesy and picture the judgment of God, much like the great Old Testament prophets. They will be killed by the Beast in Jerusalem and will be resurrected by God into heaven as their enemies look on.

4. The 144,000

   12,000 sealed saints from each of the tribes of Israel (Rev. 7:4–8)

   Pure believers in the midst of the tribulations of the last days (Rev. 14:1, 5)

(These are all individuals or specific groups of individuals. In the next session we'll look in a more comprehensive way at what will happen to believers, to the Jewish people, and to unbelievers.)

Don't forget. All of these characters play only bit parts when compared to the leading character in this drama. Never fail to give top billing to Jesus Christ.

- Jesus will _____ the Beast and his lieutenant.

  The lawless one will be revealed, whom the Lord Jesus will overthrow with the breath of his mouth and destroy by the splendor of his coming.

  —2 Thessalonians 2:8

- Jesus will redeem the two witnesses.

  Then they heard a loud voice from heaven saying to them, "Come up here." And they went up to heaven in a cloud, while their enemies looked on.

  —Revelation 11:12

- Jesus will lead the 144,000 to _____.

  They follow the Lamb wherever he goes. They were purchased from among men and offered as firstfruits to God and the Lamb.

  —Revelation 14:4

- Jesus will return in absolute _____.

  For the Lord himself will come down from heaven with a mighty shout and with the soul-stirring cry of the archangel and the great trumpet-call of God.

  —1 Thessalonians 4:16 (LB)

  Look, the Lord is coming with many thousands of his holy angels to judge every person.

  —Jude 1:14–15 (NCV)

  Look, he is coming with the clouds, and every eye will see him.

  —Revelation 1:7

  We wait for the blessed hope—the glorious appearing of our great God and Savior, Jesus Christ.

  —Titus 2:13

**Begin working on memory card 11,
"The Truth about the Second Coming."
If you haven't done them all, don't let that keep you from memorizing this one. If you've memorized each card up until now,
you will be completing a life-changing commitment.**

Discussion Questions

1. How would the fact that Jesus is coming at any moment have changed the way you faced one situation today, or how could it change the way you face one situation tomorrow?

2. Does knowing that this world will not last cause a change in your attitude toward any specific material thing, human government or institution, problem or struggle you are facing?

3. Is there anything good about knowing that things will get worse before they get better?

4. To give us hope, God has told us about some of the truths of the Second Coming of Jesus and the end of the world. Many Christians, however, feel fear when they study the Second Coming. Why do you think we feel fear? How can we move from fear to hope? Why do you think Christians who are facing persecution have always found incredible hope in the truth of Jesus' Second Coming?

Answers to Fill-Ins

responsibility	Noah's flood
curiosity	thief
hope	night
delight	soon
details	unexpected
false christs	False Prophet
don't be deceived	witnesses
apostasy	destroy
increase	victory
scoffers	glory
bridegroom	

The Second Coming
Part 2

Life Change Objective

To decide to live in anticipation of Jesus' Second Coming in one significant way this next week.

In the last session we focused on the signs of Jesus' coming, the descriptions of his coming, and some of the persons involved in the end times.

Three types of signs:

1. Signs pointing to the end (the beginning of birth pains)
2. Signs immediately preceding the end time events
3. Signs accompanying the end time events

Jesus' descriptions of the time of the Second Coming:

- Like a bridegroom
- Like the destruction of Sodom
- Like Noah's flood
- Like a thief in the night

People of the end times:

- The man of lawlessness/the Beast/the Antichrist
- A second beast/the False Prophet
- The two witnesses
- The 144,000

Never fail to give top billing to Jesus Christ.

We're now going to focus on the events of the end times and what our daily attitude toward Jesus' Second Coming should be.

Events of the End Times

It would be great to cover these events in order. Unfortunately no one agrees on the order! Before we look at some of the things that believers see from different perspectives, let's look at one thing that we all clearly agree on.

Jesus Christ is coming to this earth again

Just like he came the first time—in a visible, physical, bodily form—Jesus is coming to this earth again! Although Christians disagree about the order of events surrounding his return, of his actual return there can be no doubt. His Second Coming is spoken of even more clearly than his first coming.

> After he [Jesus] said this, he was taken up before their very eyes, and a cloud hid him from their sight. They were looking intently up into the sky as he was going, when suddenly two men dressed in white stood beside them. "Men of Galilee," they said, "why do you stand here looking into the sky? This same Jesus, who has been taken from you into heaven, will come back in the same way you have seen him go into heaven."
>
> —Acts 1:9–11

> They will see the Son of Man coming on the clouds of the sky, with power and great glory.
>
> —Matthew 24:30

> There are many rooms in my Father's house; I would not tell you this if it were not true. I am going there to prepare a place for you. After I go and prepare a place for you, I will come back and take you to be with me so that you may be where I am.
>
> —John 14:2–3 (NCV)

We're going to look at some different opinions about how this coming will take place. But don't let this study deter you from the fact that the world needs to hear: Jesus Christ is coming again!

There are four end time events that every believer needs to understand: the Tribulation, the Rapture, the visible return of Christ, and the Millennium.

The Tribulation

Revelation 4–18 describes the Tribulation in detail. The signs that accompany Jesus' Second Coming that we studied in the last session were a description of many of the occurrences in this period of tribulation. The time of Tribulation includes the Battle of Armageddon, the great final battle (Rev. 16:16).

Two characteristics will distinguish the Tribulation from other difficult times in history:

- First, it will be _____, not localized.

- Second, the Tribulation will be unique because _____ will realize and act like the end is at hand.

The Scriptures divide the seven years of the Tribulation into two equal parts. In Revelation, the two halves of the Tribulation are designated either by "time, times and half a time" (Rev. 12:14), or "forty-two months" (11:2; 13:5), or "1,260 days" (11:3; 12:6), each of which works out to three and one-half years.

Question: Will Christians go through this time of Tribulation?

In order to answer that we must first look at the event called the Rapture.

The Rapture

The title "Rapture" comes from the Latin word used in 1 Thessalonians 4:17. The original Greek word is translated "caught up" in English.

The Rapture is when Jesus gathers all believers to be with him, giving each a resurrected, glorified body. This is to be distinguished from the visible return of Jesus in which all will see him and he will judge the nations and establish his kingdom. Many see the Rapture as an event hidden to all but believers and occurring years before Jesus' visible return. Others see the Rapture and Jesus' visible return as happening simultaneously.

Although there is some question about the exact time of the Rapture (see the box at the end of this section), the questions we have about exactly when it will happen shouldn't detract from the assurance that it will happen.

First Thessalonians 4:13–18 gives the most detail about what will happen when the Lord raptures the church.

> For the Lord himself will come down from heaven, with a loud command, with the voice of the archangel and with the trumpet call of God, and the dead in Christ will rise first. After that, we who are still alive and are left will be caught up together with them in the clouds to meet the Lord in the air. And so we will be with the Lord forever. Therefore encourage each other with these words.
>
> —1 Thessalonians 4:16–18

- First: The Lord _____.

  "For the Lord himself will come down from heaven . . ."

  In the clouds (Acts 1:11). On God's conditions (Matt. 24:14). Unexpectedly (Matt. 24:37).

- Second: The dead in Christ _____.

  "And the dead in Christ will rise first . . ."

  > So will it be with the resurrection of the dead. The body that is sown is perishable, it is raised imperishable; it is sown in dishonor, it is raised in glory; it is sown in weakness, it is raised in power.
  >
  > —1 Corinthians 15:42–43

- Third: We who are alive shall be _____ with them.

  First Thessalonians 4 says, "We who are still alive and are left will be caught up together with them."

- Fourth: We _____ the Lord in the air and we will be with the Lord forever.

A Closer Look

What is the difference in timing between the Rapture of the church and the visible Second Coming of Jesus to judge the nations and set up his kingdom?

Some (amillennial and postmillennial views) regard these two as occurring one right after the other or at the same time.

Others (premillennial view) see an order. There are three general ideas as to what this order might be:

1. Pretribulation Rapture: the Rapture occurs right before the Tribulation begins.
2. Midtribulation Rapture: the Rapture occurs 3-1/2 years into the time of Tribulation.
3. Posttribulation Rapture: the Rapture occurs at the end of the seven-year Tribulation.

What should these different views say to you on a personal basis? Rejoice if God takes you out of the Tribulation of those last days. But don't be surprised, and don't lose faith if God chooses to leave us as witnesses during those last days.

The visible return of Christ

The visible return of Jesus is different from the Rapture. At his return, all the earth will see Jesus returning, and he will establish his reign and rule on the earth.

> At that time the sign of the Son of Man will appear in the sky, and all the nations of the earth will mourn. They will see the Son of Man coming on the clouds of the sky, with power and great glory.
>
> —Matthew 24:30

> Look, he is coming with the clouds, and every eye will see him, even those who pierced him; and all the peoples of the earth will mourn because of him. So shall it be! Amen.
>
> —Revelation 1:7

The Millennium

The Millennium is the term used to point to the thousand-year reign of Christ spoken of in Revelation 20:1–6.

> And I saw an angel coming down out of heaven, having the key to the Abyss and holding in his hand a great chain. He seized the dragon, that ancient serpent, who is the devil, or Satan, and bound him for a thousand years. He threw him into the Abyss, and locked and sealed it over him, to keep him from deceiving the nations anymore until the thousand years were ended. After that, he must be set free for a short time.

I saw thrones on which were seated those who had been given authority to judge. And I saw the souls of those who had been beheaded because of their testimony for Jesus and because of the word of God. They had not worshiped the beast or his image and had not received his mark on their foreheads or their hands. They came to life and reigned with Christ a thousand years. (The rest of the dead did not come to life until the thousand years were ended.) This is the first resurrection. Blessed and holy are those who have part in the first resurrection. The second death has no power over them, but they will be priests of God and of Christ and will reign with him for a thousand years.

—Revelation 20:1–6

Over the years there have arisen three major ways of looking at this thousand-year reign of Christ:

1. Postmillennial (Jesus comes again after the Millennium)

   This view holds that the kingdom of God is now being extended in the world through the preaching of the Gospel and the saving work of the Holy Spirit in the hearts of individuals. The world will eventually be Christianized, and the return of Christ will occur at the close of a long period of righteousness and peace commonly called the "Millennium." This will not be a literal 1,000 years, but actually an extended period of time.

   Strength: Optimistic view of the power of the Gospel to change the world, hope for the fulfillment of the Great Commission.

   Weakness: Practically, this view is hard to reconcile with what's happening in the world. Biblically, it is hard to reconcile with the strong teaching of the final period of tribulation.

2. Amillennial (Jesus comes again without an earthly Millennium)

   Until the end, there will be parallel development of both good and evil, God's kingdom and Satan's. After the Second Coming of Christ at the end of the world, there will be a general resurrection and general judgment of all people. The thousand-year reign of Christ is not literal; it is symbolic of Jesus' work on earth from his resurrection until his Second Coming.

   Strength: Answers questions about such things as resurrected saints living in an unregenerate world for a thousand years until the final judgment.

   Weakness: Must see a great deal of the Second Coming prophecies as spiritual symbols rather than actual events.

3. Premillennial (Jesus comes again before the Millennium)

   Premillennialism is the view that holds that the Second Coming of Christ will occur prior to the Millennium and will establish Christ's kingdom on this earth for a literal 1,000 years. The duration of Christ's kingdom will be 1,000 years. Its location will be on this earth. Its government will be the personal presence of

Christ reigning as King. And it will fulfill all the yet unfulfilled promises about Christ's earthly kingdom.

Strength: Attempts to seek understanding of all Scriptures relating to the Second Coming rather than ignoring those that are difficult to understand. A more literal view of Scripture.

Weakness: Is often marked by overcomplicated charts and with wrong guesses and differing opinions about the meaning of the symbols.

Key Personal Perspective

Four Encouragements in These Four Events

1. The truth of the Tribulation encourages me. Just because things get worse does not mean God will not soon make them better.

2. The truth of the Rapture encourages me. God will take his children home.

3. The truth of Jesus' visible return encourages me. Jesus will ultimately be Lord of all.

4. The truth of the Millennium encourages me. God has a plan that extends into eternity.

What can be seen lasts only for a time, but what cannot be seen lasts forever.

—2 Corinthians 4:18 (GNT)

At the end of time what will happen to . . .

Believers

In a word, _____!

So Christ was sacrificed once to take away the sins of many people; and he will appear a second time, not to bear sin, but to bring salvation to those who are waiting for him.

—Hebrews 9:28

And when the head Shepherd comes, your reward will be a never-ending share in his glory and honor.

—1 Peter 5:4 (NLT)

Dear friends, now we are children of God, and we have not yet been shown what we will be in the future. But we know that when Christ comes again, we will be like him, because we will see him as he really is.

—1 John 3:2 (NCV)

The Jewish people

In a word, _____.

Paul's clear statements in Romans 11 cannot be ignored.

> Again I ask: Did they stumble so as to fall beyond recovery? Not at all! Rather, because of their transgression, salvation has come to the Gentiles to make Israel envious. But if their transgression means riches for the world, and their loss means riches for the Gentiles, how much greater riches will their fullness bring! . . . I do not want you to be ignorant of this mystery, brothers, so that you may not be conceited: Israel has experienced a hardening in part until the full number of the Gentiles has come in. And so all Israel will be saved, as it is written: "The deliverer will come from Zion; he will turn godlessness away from Jacob."
>
> —Romans 11:11–12, 25–26

Unbelievers

In a word, _____.

> Then I saw a great white throne and him who was seated on it. Earth and sky fled from his presence, and there was no place for them. And I saw the dead, great and small, standing before the throne, and books were opened. Another book was opened, which is the book of life. The dead were judged according to what they had done as recorded in the books. . . . If anyone's name was not found written in the book of life, he was thrown into the lake of fire.
>
> —Revelation 20:11–12, 15

What Should Our Attitude Be?

- Be alert and _____.

Be on guard! Be alert! You do not know when that time will come.
—Mark 13:33

If he comes suddenly, do not let him find you sleeping.
—Mark 13:36

- Be alert and _____.

So then, let us not be like others, who are asleep, but let us be alert and self-controlled.
—1 Thessalonians 5:6

Therefore, prepare your minds for action; be self-controlled; set your hope fully on the grace to be given you when Jesus Christ is revealed.
—1 Peter 1:13

The end of all things is near. Therefore be clear minded and self-controlled so that you can pray.
—1 Peter 4:7

- Live holy lives.

Since everything will be destroyed in this way, what kind of people ought you to be? You ought to live holy and godly lives as you look forward to the day of God and speed its coming.

—2 Peter 3:11–12

- Be _____ and _____ wait.

You too, be patient and stand firm, because the Lord's coming is near.

—James 5:8

Therefore you do not lack any spiritual gift as you eagerly wait for our Lord Jesus Christ to be revealed.

—1 Corinthians 1:7

- Long for _____.

Now there is in store for me the crown of righteousness, which the Lord, the righteous Judge, will award to me on that day—and not only to me, but also to all who have longed for his appearing.

—2 Timothy 4:8

For the grace of God that brings salvation has appeared to all men. It teaches us to say "No" to ungodliness and worldly passions, and to live self-controlled, upright and godly lives in this present age, while we wait for the blessed hope—the glorious appearing of our great God and Savior, Jesus Christ.

—Titus 2:11–13

Key Personal Perspective

For the believer the knowledge of prophecy draws our hearts out in worship toward God. From the beginning to the end of the book of Revelation, the apostle John had a habit of responding to God's prophetic future with an attitude of worship.

When I saw him, I fell at his feet as though dead. Then he placed his right hand on me and said: "Do not be afraid. I am the First and the Last."

—Revelation 1:17

I, John, am the one who heard and saw these things. And when I had heard and seen them, I fell down to worship at the feet of the angel who had been showing them to me. But he said to me, "Do not do it! I am a fellow servant with you and with your brothers the prophets and of all who keep the words of this book. Worship God!"

—Revelation 22:8–9

There is no better summation of our study of the end times than those two powerful words of invitation, "Worship God!"

**Finish memorizing memory card 11,
"The Truth about the Second Coming."**

Appendix
Views Concerning Last Things

Categories	Amillennialism	Postmillennialism	Historic Premillennialism	Dispensational Premillennialism
Second Coming of Christ	Single event; no distinction between Rapture and Second Coming. Introduces eternal state.	Single event; no distinction between Rapture and Second Coming; Christ returns after Millennium.	Rapture and Second Coming simultaneous; Christ returns to reign on earth.	Second Coming in two phases: Rapture for church; Second Coming to earth seven years later.
Resurrection	General resurrection of believers and unbelievers at Second Coming of Christ.	General resurrection of believers and unbelievers at Second Coming of Christ.	Resurrection of believers at beginning of Millennium. Resurrection of unbelievers at end of Millennium.	Distinction in resurrections: 1. Church at Rapture 2. Old Testament/Tribulation saints at Second Coming 3. Unbelievers at end of Millennium
Judgments	General Judgment of all people	General Judgment of all people	Judgment at Second Coming Judgment at end of Tribulation	Distinction in Judgment: 1. Believers' works at Rapture 2. Jews/Gentiles at end of Tribulation 3. Unbelievers at end of Millennium
Tribulation	Tribulation is experienced in this present age.	Tribulation is experienced in this present age.	Posttribulation view: church goes through the future Tribulation.	Pretribulation view: church is raptured prior to Tribulation.
Millennium	No literal Millennium on earth after Second Coming. Kingdom present in church age.	Present age blend into Millennium because of progress of Gospel.	Millennium is both present and future. Christ is reigning in heaven, Millennium not necessarily 1,000 years.	At Second Coming Christ inaugurates literal 1,000-year Millennium on earth.
Israel and the Church	Church is the new Israel. No distinction between Israel and the church.	Some distinction between Israel and the church. Future for Israel but church is spiritual Israel.	Some distinction between Israel and the church. Future for Israel but church is spiritual Israel.	Complete distinction between Israel and church. Distinct program for each.
Adherents	L. Beckhof; O. T. Allis; G. C. Berkhouwer	Charles Hodge; B. B. Warfield; W. G. T. Shedd; A. H. Strong	G. E. Ladd; A. Reese; M. J. Erickson	L. S. Chafer; J. D. Pentecost; C. C. Ryrie; J. F. Walvoord; C. Swindoll

Source: Taken from Paul Enns, *The Moody Handbook of Theology* (Chicago: Moody Press, 1989). Used by permission.

Discussion Questions

1. What does the fact that Jesus is preparing a place for you communicate to you about his love for you? How would you like to grow in understanding the depth of Jesus' love for you?

2. Can you even imagine what the Rapture of God's church will be like? (Sort of like skydiving in reverse!) Who do you know whose resurrected body will come out of the grave to meet their spirit coming with Jesus in the air? Who would you like to clasp hands with on the way up to meet Jesus? What would you like your first thought to be when you realize what is happening?

3. What does the fact that there are so many differing opinions on subjects like the Millennium say to you?

4. Talk together about how the attitudes God teaches us to have toward the visible return of Jesus fit into our everyday lives.

   Be alert and watchful. What helps you to think about the fact that Jesus *is* going to come again?

   Be alert and self-controlled. How does the truth of the visible return of Jesus help you to say no to temptation and yes to spiritual disciplines such as prayer and serving others?

   Live holy lives. Do you live a holy life more out of fear that he will catch you doing something wrong when he returns or out of a desire to use the short time that you have to live to please the Lord? What helps you to live less with fear and more with a desire to please him?

   Be patient and eagerly wait. We all struggle with patience. What lessons have you learned (or seen in others) that help you to remember to not try to hurry God?

   Long for his return! What are you looking forward to when Jesus comes again?

For Further Study

Clouse, Robert G. *The Meaning of the Millennium.* Downers Grove, Ill.: InterVarsity Press, 1977.

Elwell, Walter, ed. *Topical Analysis of the Bible.* Grand Rapids, Mich.: Baker, 1991.

Graham, Billy. *Storm Warning.* Dallas: Word, 1992.

Lightner, Robert. *The Last Days Handbook.* Nashville: Nelson, 1990.

Little, Paul. *Know What You Believe.* Wheaton, Ill.: Victor, 1987.

Rhodes, Ron. *The Heart of Christianity.* Eugene, Ore.: Harvest House, 1996.

Answers to Fill-Ins

worldwide

all

descends

rise

caught up

meet

reward

restoration

judgment

watchful

self-controlled

patient, eagerly

his return

Wrap-Up Study

Life-Change Objective

To map out eleven personal ways you want to live the truths that we've learned together from God's Word.

> But you, dear friends, must continue to build your lives on the foundation of your holy faith.
>
> —Jude 1:20 (NLT)

> And this is my prayer: that your love may abound more and more in knowledge and depth of insight, so that you may be able to discern what is best.
>
> —Philippians 1:9–10

What Is Christian Doctrine?

Christian doctrine is an _____ of what the _____.

A working definition of theology is _____.

What Is the Value of the Doctrine You Have Learned?

1. You _____.

> We are cruel to ourselves if we try to live in this world without knowing the God whose world it is and who runs it. The world becomes a strange, mad, painful place . . . for those who don't know about God.[1]
>
> —J. I. Packer

> Let not the wise man boast of his wisdom or the strong man boast of his strength or the rich man boast of his riches, but let him who boasts boast about this: that he understands and knows me, that I am the LORD.
>
> —Jeremiah 9:23–24

2. You have _____.

In pointing out these things to the brethren, you will be a good servant of Christ Jesus, constantly nourished on the words of the faith and of the sound doctrine which you have been following.

—1 Timothy 4:6 (NASB)

3. You will be able to _____.

He must hold firmly to the trustworthy message as it has been taught, so that he can encourage others by sound doctrine and refute those who oppose it.

—Titus 1:9

4. You are protected against _____.

But solid food is for the mature, who by constant use have trained themselves to distinguish good from evil.

—Hebrews 5:14

5. You have changed the way you _____.

For as he thinks within himself, so he is.

—Proverbs 23:7 (NASB)

How a person thinks determines how they act.

6. You have built an _____.

Therefore leaving the elementary teaching about the Christ, let us press on to maturity, not laying again a foundation of repentance from dead works and of faith toward God, of instruction [doctrine] about washings [baptism], and laying on of hands, and the resurrection of the dead, and eternal judgment.

—Hebrews 6:1–2 (NASB)

The Foundation of My Life Is Determined By:

1. Where I set my heart

   Since, then, you have been raised with Christ, set your hearts on things above, where Christ is seated at the right hand of God.
   —Colossians 3:1

2. Where I set my mind

   Set your minds on things above, not on earthly things.
   —Colossians 3:2

   They love the LORD's teachings, and they think about those teachings day and night.
   —Psalm 1:2 (NCV)

   Brothers and sisters, think about the things that are good and worthy of praise. Think about the things that are true and honorable and right and pure and beautiful and respected.
   —Philippians 4:8 (NCV)

3. Where I fix my eyes

   Let us fix our eyes on Jesus, the author and perfecter of our faith, who for the joy set before him endured the cross, scorning its shame, and sat down at the right hand of the throne of God.
   —Hebrews 12:2

   So we fix our eyes not on what is seen, but on what is unseen. For what is seen is temporary, but what is unseen is eternal.
   —2 Corinthians 4:18

Father,

Thank you for showing us the truth in your Word, through your Son and by your Spirit. Our heartfelt request is that the truths we have learned will be lived out in our daily lives. We make this request in confidence, knowing you want us to be doers of your Word. But we also ask this humbly. Lord, we can't live your truth on our own strength: although that hasn't kept us from falling flat on our faces trying! We need, desperately need, your presence and power in our lives. Through that power we pray that you will enable us to build our lives on the foundation of your truth.

In Jesus' name, amen.

Building a Foundation That Lasts

Three Levels of Truth

Here's a brief look at what we've studied together these past few months. This chart helps you to see the different levels of learning that go along with grasping a truth. Being able to quote a truth does not mean I've fully grasped that truth.

To grasp a doctrine I must . . .	Learn It (understand the truth)	Love It (change my perspective)	Live It (apply it to life)
The Bible	The Bible is God's perfect guidebook for living.	I can make the right decision.	I will consult the Bible for guidance in my decision about _____.
God	God is bigger and better and closer than I can imagine.	The most important thing about me is what I believe about God.	When I see how great God is, it makes _____ look small.
Jesus	Jesus is God showing himself to us.	God wants me to know him better.	I will get to know Jesus through a daily quiet time.
The Holy Spirit	God lives in me and through me now.	I am a temple of God's Holy Spirit.	I will treat my body like the temple it is by _____.
Creation	Nothing "just happened." God created it all.	I have a purpose in this world.	The reason I exist is to _____.
Salvation	Grace is the only way to have a relationship with God.	I am an object of God's grace.	I'll stop seeing _____ as a way to earn my salvation. I'll begin doing it simply in appreciation for God's grace.
Sanctification	Faith is the only way to grow as a believer.	I grow when I see myself in a new way.	I'll spend more time listening to what God's Word says about me and less time listening to what the world says about me.
Good and Evil	God has allowed evil to provide us with a choice. God can bring good even out of evil events. God promises victory over evil to those who choose him.	All things work together for good.	I am battling evil as I face _____. I will overcome evil with good by _____.
The Afterlife	Heaven and hell are real places. Death is a beginning, not the end.	I can face death with confidence.	I will have a more hopeful attitude toward _____.
The Church	The only true "world superpower" is the church.	The best place to invest my life is in God's church.	I need to make a deeper commitment to the church by _____.
The Second Coming	Jesus is coming again to judge this world and to gather God's children.	I want to be living alertly for him when he comes.	Someone I can encourage with the hope of the Second Coming is _____.

Answers to Fill-Ins

organized summary

Bible teaches

faith seeking understanding

know God better

fed your soul

share with others

error

think

essential foundation

Notes

Introductory Study

1. J. I. Packer, *Truth and Power* (Wheaton, Ill.: Shaw, 1996), 16.

Session 1. The Bible: Part 1

1. Norman L. Geisler and Ronald M. Brooks, *When Skeptics Ask* (Wheaton, Ill.: Victor, 1990), 159–60.

2. William F. Albright, *The Archaeology of Palestine*, (Harmondsworth, Middlesex: Pelican, 1960), 127.

3. Josh McDowell, *Evidence That Demands a Verdict* (San Bernardino, Calif.: Here's Life Publishers, 1972), 19–20.

4. Geisler and Brooks, *When Skeptics Ask*, 145.

Session 3. God: Part 1

1. A. W. Tozer, *Knowledge of the Holy* (New York: Harper and Row, 1961), 9.

2. J. P. Moreland, Saddleback Church men's retreat, 7 February 2000.

Session 4. God: Part 2

1. Billy Graham, *The Holy Spirit: Activating God's Power in Your Life* (New York: Warner, 1980), 27–28.

Session 5. Jesus: Part 1

1. Walter Elwell, ed., *Topical Analysis of the Bible* (Grand Rapids, Mich.: Baker, 1991).

2. *Encyclopaedia Britannica*, 15th ed., s.v. "Jesus Christ."

Session 6. Jesus: Part 2

1. C. S. Lewis, *Mere Christianity* (New York: Macmillan, 1952), 55–56.

2. Josh McDowell, *Evidence That Demands a Verdict* (San Bernadino, Calif.: Here's Life Publishers, 1979), 103–7.

3. Peter W. Stoner, *Science Speaks: Scientific Proof of the Accuracy of Prophecy and the Bible*, 3rd rev. ed. (Chicago: Moody Press, 1969), 100–107.

Session 8. The Holy Spirit: Part 2

1. The following three illustrations are taken from *The Spirit-Filled Life*, used by permission from Campus Crusade for Christ.

Session 9. Creation: Part 1

1. R. E. D. Clark, *Darwin: Before and After* (London: Paternoster, 1948), 86.

2. Francis Crick, *Life Itself, Its Origin and Nature* (New York: Simon and Schuster, 1981), 51–52.

3. Charles C. Ryrie, *Basic Theology* (Wheaton, Ill.: SP Publications, 1986), 177.

4. Fred Hoyle, *The Intelligent Universe* (New York: Holt, Rinehart and Winston, 1983), 19.

5. Francis Darwin, *Life and Letters of Charles Darwin* (New York: Basic Books, 1959), 1: 210.

6. David Raup, "Conflicts Between Darwin and Paleontology," *Field Museum of Natural History Bulletin* 30, no. 1 (1979): 25.

7. Michael J. Behe, *Darwin's Black Box: The Biochemical Challenge to Evolution* (New York: Free Press, 1995), 39.

8. Gregory Koukl, *Michael Behe's Theistic Evolution,* transcript of Stand to Reason Radio, 24 December 1997, accessed 1 February 2003 at www.str.org.

9. Dr. Ray Bohlin, *Why We Believe in Creation.* Accessed 1 February 2003 at www.probe.org.

10. Michael D. Lemonick, "Echoes of the Big Bang," *Time,* (4 May 1992), 62.

11. Sharon Begley, "Science Finds God," *Newsweek* (20 July 1998): 46–51.

12. Robert Jastrow, *God and the Astronomers,* 2d ed. (New York: W. W. Norton, 1992), 106–7.

Session 12. Salvation: Part 2

1. The three bulleted points were adapted from Charles C. Ryrie, *So Great Salvation* (Wheaton, Ill.: Victor, 1989), 142–43.

2. Appendix adapted and abridged from Charles Stanley, *Eternal Security: Can You Be Sure?* (Nashville: Nelson, 1990), 135–83.

Session 15. Good and Evil: Part 1

1. Aleksandr I. Solzhenitsyn, *The Gulag Archipelago, 1918–1956,* trans. Thomas P. Whitney (New York: Harper & Row, 1985), 615.

Session 16. Good and Evil: Part 2

1. C. S. Lewis, *The Problem of Pain* (New York: Macmillan, 1962), 93.

Session 18. The Afterlife: Part 2

1. Source unknown.

Session 21. The Second Coming: Part 1

1. Billy Graham, *Approaching Hoofbeats: The Four Horsemen of the Apocalypse* (Waco, Tex.: Word, 1983), 19–20.

2. Charles R. Swindoll, *Growing Deep in the Christian Life* (Portland, Ore.: Multnomah Press, 1986), 268.

3. Graham, *Approaching Hoofbeats,* 23.

Wrap-Up Study

1. J. I. Packer, *Truth and Power* (Wheaton, Ill.: Shaw, 1996), 16.

Resources Available

Audiotapes of Foundations. Audiotapes of each of the *Foundations* studies, taught by Tom Holladay and Kay Warren, are available at www.pastors.com.

Purpose-Driven Church. This award-winning book by Rick Warren shows how your church can help people live God's five purposes for our lives. Available in book and DVD in twenty languages. Millions of people have studied this book in churches and groups. (Zondervan)

Purpose-Driven Life. Rick Warren takes the groundbreaking message of the award-winning *Purpose-Driven Church* and goes deeper, applying it to the lifestyle of individual Christians. *The Purpose-Driven Life* is a manifesto for Christian living in the twenty-first century: a lifestyle based on eternal purposes, not cultural values. Written in a captivating devotional style, the book is divided into forty short chapters that can be read as a daily devotional, studied by small groups, and used by churches participating in a 40 Days of Purpose campaign. (Zondervan)

40 Days of Purpose. A forty-day campaign for churches that builds on *The Purpose-Driven Life* as a foundation, adding sermons, small group resources and video tapes, and training for leadership teams. This is a forty-day emphasis that promises to permanently change your church. (contact PurposeDriven.com)

Purpose-Driven Youth Ministry. The essentials of a healthy, purpose-driven youth ministry from Saddleback's youth pastor, Doug Fields. (Zondervan)

Pastors.com and PurposeDriven.com have additional resources for those in full-time ministry. Pastors.com specializes in messages and helps for the pastor as a communicator, including sermons and books. PurposeDriven.com specializes in tools and program materials to help churches focus on our God-given purposes.